Off-the-Wall Wa

Sing to me of the man, Muse, the man of twists and turns
driven time and again off course

Homer: The Odyssey
(translated by Robert Fagles)

Best wishes

Laurence Shelley

Off-the-Wall Walking

A different kind of journey

by

LAURENCE SHELLEY

with wood engravings by
HILARY PAYNTER

and line illustrations by
GERRARD LINDLEY

First published by Thetis Publications in 2007
Reprinted 2008

British Library Cataloguing-in-Publication Data
A catalogue record for this book is available
from the British Library

ISBN 978-0-9556750-0-3

Wood engravings © Hilary Paynter
Line illustrations by Gerrard Lindley
Back cover photograph by Laurence Shelley
Cover and interior design by Terence Sackett

Printed and bound by Lazarus Press
Unit 7 Caddsdown Business Park
Bideford Devon EX39 3DX
www.lazaruspress.com

Published by
Thetis Publications
60 Bay View Road
Northam Bideford
Devon EX39 1BH
Tel/Fax 01237 424424

email: laurence@thetispublications.co.uk
www.thetispublications.co.uk

For Lielee

ACKNOWLEDGEMENTS

At the end of this walk was the challenge of another journey – the writing and publication of this book. Thanks from the bottom of my boots to the support team: to my family who've been with me every inch of the way; to all those who tended the path and told me where I stumbled – Graham Fawcett, Susie Barrett for the Calyx Centre infusions, Crysse Morrison, Helen Jagger Wood and everyone at Indian King's; to Marian Van Eyk McCain and the Hartland Writers' Circle for the refreshment always provided and to the Bideford writers – Philip Jones, Miranda Cox, Claire Bowles (with us in spirit), Pauline Smith and Terence Sackett – for being close enough to give a push when I needed it and canny enough for the touch of restraint when I thought I didn't. A special thanks to Terence for his guidance and expertise on presentation.

The collaboration with Hilary Paynter and Gerrard Lindley on the illustrations has been a particular pleasure and privilege. My thanks wouldn't be complete without embracing all the fellow travellers who made this the walk it was, especially Pat and Sue, the blister angels, and never forgetting the sandal saviours, Eileen and Geoff. As for Caracalla who started this whole thing off, I can only hope that some good has come out of him at last.

CREDITS

'Book 1: Athena Inspires the Prince' by Homer, from *The Odyssey* by Homer, translated by Robert Fagles, copyright ©1996 by Robert Fagles. Used by permission of Viking Penguin, a division of Penguin Group (USA) Inc.

Ian McMillan for permission to use the extract from *I Found This Shirt*, Carcanet Press Limited, 1998.

Catherine Tennant for the extract from the *Daily Telegraph* magazine section, 12th July 2003. Permission applied for.

Tullie House Museum and Art Gallery for permission to use the transcriptions from *The Whispering Wall* by Stephen Skrynka.

Bart Simpson for his socks.

FOREWORD

FOUR WORDS

'I never liked him.'

That was all the woman beside me said. I was in the Metropolitan Museum, New York on my way to an American art exhibition, but one face had stopped me dead among twenty or so Roman busts. The woman's words confirmed my suspicions. I looked again. An emperor stared back – Caracalla – callous and grim. What was there to never like? Practically everything, I discovered. And the more I read, the more life in Roman times had me hooked.

That was how this journey started.

When Hadrian's Wall Path opened, it was a great opportunity to follow in Roman footsteps. I allowed six days to walk the 84 miles; ample time, I thought, to take in some Roman sites along the way. It seemed a straightforward target. My direction proved anything but straight.

Why? I should have guessed from New York. Intent on American art, I'd bought into Roman history instead. If one look and four words took me off course, how easily might I be diverted by other chance events? I didn't know it then, but I played into the hands of providence beautifully, with an early departure from common sense.

THE OUTSET

'Boundaries are always challenged'

I GOOD BUY

Why do I always leave things to the last minute? The day before and I'm still shopping for decent walking boots. The first pair does nothing for my country cred. Another pair threatens the skin on my shins. The third pair looks the part, fits like a glove and at £39.95p it's a snip. When the assistant throws in thick socks, I lift off. A bargain like this must be a good omen.

It's a personal challenge: to walk Hadrian's Wall Path east to west, from near Newcastle to well beyond Carlisle, a modest enough goal in six days, but the furthest I'll have walked. I've fixed up accommodation for all but the last two nights and I admit it; I'm like a kid who's broken up for the holidays, raring to let off steam.

On the train from Barnstaple to Exeter, the gentle folds of Devon hills flit past, tractor tramlines criss-cross fields of wheat and mist flirts with a river valley. But where am I? Far away, in a landscape less forgiving, with breathtaking space and profound silence. I picture myself marching with a sense of history, along the path of the Wall which defined the northern limits of the Roman Empire and helped defend its gains. Boundaries are always challenged.

I am on the Virgin Voyager to Newcastle now. And boy, it's hot. 'We apologise for the breakdown in air-conditioning' is all we get. Everyone is shiny. Noses are red. Some are dripping. 'Due to a technical hitch, we regret we cannot provide hot drinks.' The bad news is there are no refrigerated drinks either.

I observe on the unopenable window that we are in the quiet zone. We are periodically reminded over the speaker, 'no mobile phones, no loud talking'. 'Sit back and relax' a sticker urges. It might well add 'and quietly suffocate'.

II VIRGIN REBIRTH

I have the misfortune to be on the inside of an elderly woman, wearing an unbelievably unsuitable dark blue mackintosh that never had any life in it, but is currently stifling my left flank. It never enters her head to take it off. Apart from mopping her brow twice she seems impervious to the heat, while the rampant sweat breaking out of my every pore feels like the full flow of a tropical fever.

She tells me how much she enjoyed her holiday in Ilfracombe and that this is her first train ride in thirty years. Where has she been? I can't help observing the white stubble on her chin and the NHS-type glasses we called goggles because kids looked like they were in goldfish bowls. Her white hair is a riot of independently-minded curls, grey at the back as if reverting to some past glory. She really is the least fashionable pensioner I have ever met. I'm thinking of Captain Mainwaring in drag when she starts on a Corporal Jones reminiscence. It's too much. I'm a sitting target. If I don't expire from heat exhaustion next to her mac, I'll die from over-exposure to her family history. 'Do excuse me,' I say. 'Nature calls.'

She has done me a favour. Bending the Retail Service Manager's ear over the counter, I find a coolish bottle of *Cristaline Eau de Source* spring water in my hand. More critically, I elicit the priceless information that the air-conditioning is working in coach B. Provided I move before Birmingham, I will get a spare seat.

The situation is utterly transformed. Now I know what it is like to bathe in a mountain stream. I enter a different world.

People are matt-faced. They have up-to-the-minute haircuts and mobiles with catchy call-tunes. They are making entries in diaries, talking loudly about matters of moment and reading top-ten novels through designer specs. These are the movers and shakers of rail trips, those who condition themselves for the Virgin Rebirth. I feel more at home already.

III WITHIN REACH

The androgynous lady gets off at Birmingham New Street wheeling her suitcase, carrying a Sainsbury's bag and a backpack that must be full of family archives. She's a camel with too many humps. Even her coat has a hood. She has the look of someone whose meaning was misconstrued during some terrible mix-up in the maternity ward. I am unkind. No doubt.

I settle back in more charitable mind to view the enormous crop of chickweed and Wimpy/Barratt homes lining the trackside north of Birmingham.

Argos, pylons and Floors 2 Go,
Briggs of Burton,
Warehouse, ripe for loft conversion,
Volvo truck depot,
Kerry Foods, Etoile Dancewear,
Ewart Chainbelt Co.
Quay Plastics, React Fast,
All sweep past.
There's purpose now.
To the North
And Hadrian's Wall we go

Time to read the *Daily Telegraph*. I turn to the magazine section and idly, as one does, see what the stars have in store. Here, Taurus: *'If a goal has seemed beyond your reach, all that is due to change from Sunday, when the Full Moon gives you extra insight and determination. But if you are to make the most of this week's chances, you need to give yourself more freedom'.* Catherine Tennant, thanks. I'm ready for that extra insight. I know what I'll do: I'll notice what I notice.

And when I arrive, where better to start than the Baltic Centre for Contemporary Art at Gateshead? One image impresses me: a photograph of a disintegrating miner's boot, all grey and white, embedded in cracked clay. Is that what a way of life comes to?

Then I see Antony Gormley's disembodied sculptures. Moulds from more than 250 people were used to create welded networks of steel bars, new skeletal forms which evoke the spirit within flesh and bone. A frivolous youth gives one reconstructed figure a tweak, setting off an alarming vibration. It continues twitching until steadied by an attendant. I reflect on what we leave behind; an old boot in cracked clay, or maybe just a twitch.

IV INSIDE STORY

On to my first B & B at Wallsend and nothing can prepare me for what lies inside the unpretentious exterior of this Victorian mid-terrace house. I step through the front door and step back one century. I am greeted by a dark-suited gentleman, Colin, but more so by a rich, ruby-red carpet and flickering chandelier. Umbrellas stand to attention in customary shell-case. A gracious lady plays a drawing room piano on the wall.

'This is the breakfast room,' Colin announces in his master-of-ceremonies voice (a northern brogue with shades of the Welsh borders) that carries all the way to an Arab boy holding a candelabrum and sends shivers round a glass-tasselled lamp. Up the stairs we go, patterns flying everywhere: below the dado and to the heavens above. Mercifully, the ceiling and woodwork are plain coloured: that authentic combination of faded cream and brown.

In the lounge next, with its choirboys, winged maidens and a fair-skinned nymph on a pedestal bearing a robe, but still baring two plump breasts. There are Staffordshire dogs in the hearth of the marble-veined fireplace and hunting men with scurrying chickens round about. A candle of ecclesiastical proportions begs to be lit. It is dark, but my eyes light up when Colin says, 'Do help yourself to a complimentary glass of sherry.' There's port and Madeira too, just the tonic to replenish the flow of liquid from my nasal orifice as the cold takes hold. Retribution for some unkind thoughts, perhaps? But the Madeira is top hole, so good that I sample a second glass to be sure.

'Apologies,' Colin enunciates. 'Your en-suite room is not in commission. A single person put the shower out of action and much else besides. The damage will take two days to repair.'

'What exactly did he do?'

Colin brushes aside my probing. 'I couldn't possibly go into detail,' he says, which makes me think worse of it, but he speaks without rancour. 'It's only happened once in twenty years. I'll send him the bill.'

Colin is a period piece of repose. His world is in equilibrium and no more finely calculated than in the bathroom. 'The wallpaper is designed by Charles Gibson' a plaque relates. His Gibson girls 'epitomised the American ideal of femininity at the turn of the century'. Colin was lucky enough to find four rolls of the esteemed paper in a North Shields junk shop, just enough to do the bathroom. I feel privileged to have a bath surrounded by two hundred Gibson girls, all thankfully looking sideways.

No half measures for Colin. There's a *Gucci Pour Homme* jar which must hold pints of the stuff. It takes two hands to lift. And I am bemused to see a neat line of dark green braid bordering the tiles above the bath. Who else would have thought of that? But the Llewelyn-Bowen moment soon passes.

The bedrooms have names like Bewick, after the celebrated wood engraver, or Dobson and Grainger, other local notables. Downstairs, one room is elevated to The Lord Collingwood Suite. My room is not in that league. Perhaps the savage attack scuppered my chances. The good Lord might not appreciate the stick-on film masquerading as stained glass on the windows.

He'd be finicky. And so would I, for I am blessed with a bottle of mouthwash, cookies to take with a herbal tea selection, and one handmade slice of Northumberland fruit cake.

A Pre-Raphaelite print features naked women disporting themselves in a lily pond, with an Adonis-like youth ministering from the edge. I cannot feel hard done by. Ministering to naked ladies in lily ponds must be the stuff of dreams. I sleep well.

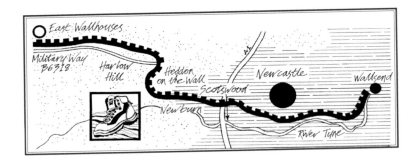

DAY ONE

'It's a long road I'm on. How can I shorten it?'

V TOUGH TARGET

It's 7.30 a.m., a rude time to be having breakfast on a Sunday but I want to be off early. My first day is to take me through Newcastle to a village called East Wallhouses. I need to make good headway but twenty miles is a tough target on what looks like one of the hottest days.

The strains of baroque music from the orchestra, cunningly concealed under a well-draped table, fail to detach apprehension from the anticipation. In my pocketed shorts and bound-up boots, I feel out of joint with the Arab boy and his candelabrum. And why, I don't know, but I dwell on the shower incident. What about all the dark Transylvanian secrets a house like this might hold? A bellyful of scrambled egg, tomato, mushrooms and sautéed potatoes, and I'm easily reassured.

I ask Colin about his Imperial Ground Coffee Blend.

'It's unique, you know; blended specially for us. We fiddled for weeks trying hundreds of combinations. Apart from Brazil – you can't avoid Brazil – it had to be ex-Empire, so there are beans from Uganda, Honduras and Mysore.'

'I'll take a packet,' I say, and with it the conviction that the past is best left behind; learned from, not lived in. You can't carry on regardless and you shouldn't ignore the shower vandal. That's how it starts. Attack Roman bathhouses and you'd undermine an Empire. Even one disguised as a Victorian mid-terrace isn't safe.

VI SHORT NOTICE

I've started. At 8.35 a.m. I stride past the Swan Hunter shipyard. There's something archaeological about the welded girders which function as seats on the path. I meet a chap walking the other way.

'Hallo,' I say.

'All right,' he replies affirmatively, as though I'd asked and he was.

I am entertained by this shorthand speak. It reminds me of the Barnsley man ordering fish and chips, as recounted by Ian McMillan. 'Once,' Barnsley man says, meaning one fish and chips. I love the sheer economy. It tells me about northerners; how they like to get on with it, no bush-beating.

Then I spot, amongst the graffiti on a warehouse wall, 'Angelic Upstarts OK'. With a name like that, they can't be that bad, can they? It's brightened up the wall. It's brightened me too. I feel infected. A certain jauntiness takes over and I do something I've never done before; turn my baseball cap back to front. Wow! First, a walker. Now, with attitude. And, if anyone asks, 'all right?', I'm ready.

'It's to shield my neck from the sun,' I'll say, or more probably, 'Neck shield, see'. But they won't, will they? Ask, I mean. All young chaps wear baseball caps the wrong way round. It's just that I'm not young … yet. But they won't know. In fact, seeing me back to front, they won't even guess. And there's another reason.

Things are looking up, when a run of broken glass on the path draws my eyes down. It's my new noticing mode. Nasty, I think. But then, not so nasty perhaps, from the glass breaker's viewpoint. It's the sort of thing any 'Angelic Upstart' might do for want of anything better; like not being able to play the broken organ that I'm passing.

Can you blame him? The breaking of a bottle has much to commend it. There's the co-ordination of hand and eye as he takes aim, the release of emotion as he throws and the sensual pleasure – visual and aural, don't forget – as the bottle shatters. If we are to object, it might be about the difficulty of recycling or the loss to the tactile sense when pieces are not picked up.

It is this 'not picking up', I now realise, that gave rise to the 'nasty' thought. This, and the fact that I have to sidestep the shards, just before a passing cyclist swerves to avoid the same. 'Puncture' flashes into my head. Where *do* my telepathic powers come from? Rounding the next corner, I see the same cyclist inspecting a deflated tyre. Nothing supernatural really. It's what you expect. The very things we desperately avoid happen: like babies and a nose that runs when you walk.

'But I saw you swerve,' I mutter as I pass by.

'No, it weren't that. It were further back. You get punctures all the time 'ere,' he says.

There you have it. You can't relax. You have to be vigilant when you're noticing; now, before and after.

Soon after, I notice that a notice which once read 'Investing in the Environment' is almost completely invested with graffiti. But, at 9.15 a.m., I notice a rabbit. And, just after the rabbit scoots, I don't. I notice, a bare 40 minutes after my walk started, a blister.

VII PREPOSTEROUS THOUGHTS

'Blasted blister,' I bleat pathetically. And where is *my* repair kit? I explore the options; something to cushion the inflating balloon that is my right heel; a sponge if I have one. I don't. And then, the most preposterous lateral thinking; sponge … cake. Yes, what about that Northumberland fruit cake I brought with me? Messy, perhaps, but the sultanas and glaciated cherries might do the trick. No. The look on Colin's face would haunt the rest of my days.

Well, of course, there is always the plaster, a few patches of which my dear wife had the prescience to pack, only a little smaller than the blister my right heel is bent on developing. But how do you plaster a balloon? The logistics send me into a back alley of questions I've never thought to ask, such as; you can't possibly keep nailing horseshoes in the same holes can you or they wouldn't stay put? A subset of questions centres round layers of skin. Can I really draw on another six, when this one's gone? I am appalled at my ignorance but stick a plaster on best as I can and make the most of what grass is left to ease my approach to Newcastle.

Walking by the banks of the Tyne is some consolation for the growing tarmac. So are the antics of local jokers. 'Relax ... you're moving to Trinity Court' an estate agent's board reassures, alongside a photo of a life-threatening bear. Over the photo is scrawled 'This is Simon Court', a home-grown predator that home buyers ought to find more unsettling. Outside a pub at a marina, a blackboard advertises Fosters at £2 a pint but 50p a half. Keep to halves, I say, until I realise that an enterprising finger has erased the £1 that preceded it. Ah well.

Temptation deferred, I divert the nagging heel with different walking styles. I try a tiptoe progression, but that must look as if I'm about to creep up on someone and say 'boo' or worse. A whole sole tread produces a strange, gliding motion. But it makes me feel I've joined a mystic sect which wears long cloaks and floats just above the ground. This would suit me fine right now, except that heel first, though uncomfortable, is least likely to get me arrested. I settle for a limp, but hallucinate a solution. The ambulance I convince myself is in front, though, turns out to be a motorhome.

VIII BAND PRACTICE

Truth to tell, I'm not that bad a case, physically that is. But the mind is a wonderful misinterpreter, so it comes as some relief to discover that the surreal tinkling in my ears now is not of my imagining. Round the bend, I see real drums and a xylophone ringing out *'Alexander's Ragtime Band'*. It's a band on a Sunday morning practice, with the very sounds to get me going.

Following the river, I stride out on a wave of enthusiasm. All it takes is a busker strumming *'Blowing in the Wind'* to waft me along to the Quayside Open Air Market.

As I hip-hop past the stalls, my noticing moves into a higher gear. I know I need plasters. But how is it that, out of all the stalls I pass, I'm stopped in my tracks by one selling whole lengths of it? Two and a half feet lengths, in language my feet understand. And only 50p a time. I buy one, think better of it and buy two. Now I have five feet of the stuff, enough to get well and truly plastered.

IX PINK LADIES

Then my ears are bent by a barrow boy of Victor Mature years.

'Look 'ere. Bumper pack of fruit. Only two quid. See what you get: pound of bananas, five nectarines, a melon, five oranges and four Pink Ladies. You can't beat that. All for two quid.'

'Pink Ladies – I know – apples. Had 'em in New York,' I retort. 'Flew 'em in specially, did you?'

He's amused. 'Yeah, we got contacts. D'ya see *Grease*? They're in that.'

'Had a starring role, did they?' I banter.

'You bet. Should be in the papers, what we do. It's a steal at this price.'

I don't know what comes over me, but I'm a man possessed. Standing in front of the stall, I shout the good news. 'C'mon now. You'll never see this again. Unbelievable. It's a cri-em not to buy 'em. All this,' with a flourish at the fruit, 'for two quid.'

Two not very pink ladies give me a strange look and hurry on. 'I tried,' I say. 'Tell you what, I can't take the lot – too loaded up – but if you can do four Pink Ladies for 50p you're on.' I'm on, and off. Four juicy Pink Ladies should help see me through the heat of the day.

Just as I'm thinking I'd better get a move on, I'm arrested ... by trays full of socks, all in packs of three for £2-99. One pair of thin socks would do fine for cushioning my thickish pair. A shake of the head. They don't do singles. But a brainwave; my man produces a tray of clearance socks. And yes, he'll do a pair for £1 ... with Bart Simpson on. OK, I'm not proud. The market might have ambushed me and I've lost twenty minutes, valuable time. But look what I come away with: a feeling that I can hack anything, even Bart Simpson clambering up my legs.

X   WRONG TRACK?

That stands me in good stead. The Hadrian's Wall Path signs have disappeared and I'm equipped with the scantiest of maps. Heading on, still by the river, I have that uneasy sense that I'm on the wrong track. A rat scuttling into the bushes doesn't help. But people are very helpful, telling me they don't know the way either, so I entertain myself by researching the graffiti this side of Newcastle.

The creative spark is still fizzing. Over the slightly dented metal bars of a riverside seat, the motto 'No Dance. No Life' is dabbed on, a sentiment I could well subscribe to. A little further, on the next seat, the graffiti artist's message is more dubious: 'No Dents. More Dobs'. No dents indeed but, to add to the dobs of letters, some brown spots. It looks as though he's used acid to etch a rusty look into the metal.

Passing to a third seat, I come to his farewell statement: 'No Dross. No Weekend', with a lot more dobs. Now unless we're talking dope, 'dross' must mean that no weekend is complete without some scummy act. I dread to think what that might be; a long way from the 'No Dance. No Life' sentiment, for sure.

I don't want to make too much of this, but do I sense something profound? Clearly the three seats have been planned in sequence, to be read forward or back. Going my way, I'm heading for decline and fall. But anyone approaching Newcastle would be on course for the dawn and rise ... of civilisation, naturally. The man's a genius and these seats are sculptures worthy of the Baltic Centre. They must be. Though my heel is trying very hard to get in on the act, I don't sit on any of them.

XI THINKING OUTSIDE

Anyway, the graffiti has done its job. My musings have occupied my mind. I'm a lot further down the river but it really is time I listen to my right foot. I re-dress my blister on an unembellished seat with a generous length of plaster, stretching in a big 'U' from below one shin, across the blister and up to the shin on the other side. It's impressive, if I say so myself, and I'm so pleased with my nursing proficiency badge that I treat the other foot the same, just in case. Then it's the Bart Simpson's, before pulling the original socks back on.

The sun's well up in the sky now and I'm ready for action. One small thing though: where the bloody hell is Hadrian's Wall Path? One chap wants me to head away from the river to some place called Newburn. Sounds right to me. It *is* warm. I'll try it.

Uncertainty makes a muckle out of a mile. Where are the blasted signs? I'm taunted by others. One hoarding reads, 'They said it couldn't be done'. Of course it can. Another, for Vodaphone, urges 'thinking outside the box'. Well, I'm certainly outside. It's a long road I'm on. How can I shorten it? A book I read recounted the story of a man who found money when he was in a happy state of mind; lying in the street – the money, that is – and not in other people's pockets.

A wire fence borders the pavement. Swept against it are the scraps all human life has dispensed with. Could it be ... could it possibly be that among these scraps is hidden a little treasure, like a five pound note? Would anyone look for a five pound note in the company of old sweet wrappers and fag packets? Of course not. But, thinking outside of any box, I do. I look. Believe me, I look.

[DAY ONE]

I find a delivery note for timber that got delivered without a delivery note, a parking ticket that got parked where it shouldn't, lots of flyers that flew and pages from *The Sun* that have mostly landed in the gutter. But, has a five pound note sailed out of a passing car? Not one. Not even a compromising love note as a consolation prize. Anyway, I am rewarded. Ahead I see a sign to Newburn and, a little further, strike gold: a Hadrian's Wall Path sign. Scotswood, it reads. It's 11.25 and I'm back on track. I celebrate my good fortune with my first Pink Lady. Delicious!

XII ROLLING UP

The force is with me. Even as I walk the next section, a helpful woman with an Alsatian minder warns, 'You can't get through. It's blocked ahead because of the burnt-out cars. Go round past The Sporting Arms.' But when I reach what I think is The Sporting Arms, it sports no name. That's disappeared. So too has the pub. All it offers is full board … over every window.

Path closed, pub closed, vandals … what is the world coming to? While I contemplate the sad sight, some passing cyclists shout the way on, without my even asking. 'Up the hill. Through a gap in the hedge. On the left. You'll see.' Then they're gone. Cycling. Now that's much quicker.

The gap leads me into some parkland where, small wonder, my eyes light on handlebars in long grass. I wander over in that disinterested way one has of approaching something that could be free for the taking, especially if unobserved. Shame. It's a kid's bike and twisted wheels tell all … about the choice I don't have to make.

So when, a few yards on, I spy a small tyred wheel, it's only natural, isn't it, to pick it up and admire the symmetry of something so untwisted; perfect, one might say, circumferentially. And so handily sized too to … well, let go, with a little run, to see it roll … extremely roundly.

Such is my interest in the rolling business that, when I recover the wheel, I realise how little I had been aware of the time I took to get there. Unwittingly, it seems, I have hit upon my own walker incentive scheme.

This is how it works:
1. Roll the wheel
2. Follow its course
3. Pick it up
4. Be unaware of distance covered
5. Repeat 1 to 4 indefinitely.
Result: distance accomplished indefinitely.

XIII ON TRIAL

Trouble is that a wheel rolled, uncontrolled, goes anywhere but straight. It's like bowling with so much bias that the ball's positively prejudiced. As with all sport, there's a technique to be learned, a skill to be refined. But I've cracked it. It's simple. When, as a kid, I wanted a hoop to return to me (talk about dated!), I'd throw it in the air with a reverse spin. With practice, straight back it would come, good as gold. For forward projection, the technique only needs a tweak; throw the wheel low and long, with more of a reverse jerk than spin, to act as a brake on landing. The wheel then scuds off in a straightforward direction. That's the theory.

It takes some time to hone the skill. The delivery is paramount; keeping the wheel vertical at the moment of release. Having turned a corner, ready to repeat the exercise, I am passed by a young bloke with a briefcase. I can't risk a direct hit, can I, or his opprobrium? No. I postpone my next trial until he's safely gone.

Now will do. I try again. Perfect. The wheel comes to a halt at the turning to a bridge which briefcase man has just crossed. That's my path too. But the noise is deafening. The bridge spans a busy dual carriageway, the A1 indeed, in a shallow arc. What if … the thought occurs … I get the wheel to land halfway? Then it will run down the slope. And if it overtakes him, or flops at his feet – a wheel out of nowhere – it won't matter what he thinks. On this side, out of sight, I wouldn't be seen. Fun, really.

XIV LACKING CONVICTION

I aim and, ready with the jerk, throw. In that instant, I realise it's all going horribly wrong. Instead of long and low, the throw is short and high. Instead of ahead, my throw is going … over the effing edge of the parapet, straight on to the road below. Horror-struck, I rush to the side. It's in mid-air. The wheel is spinning, hanging there. Hope … despair. Traffic's everywhere.

Newspaper headlines are written all over me. 'KID'S WHEEL CAUSES PILE-UP' … 'TRAGIC DEATHS'. I close my eyes to the number killed and injured. A sub-head reads, '*He wore baseball cap back to front*'. It goes on, '*Key witness, Oliver Leggitt (of law firm Hackles & Frogham) stated, "He was behaving strangely – disturbed I'd say – throwing the wheel all over the place." Police are looking for an oldish man, white bearded, wearing khaki shorts, carrying a rucksack and with a pronounced limp.*'

Never mind the rest of it, there's no way I can disguise the limp. I don't stand a chance. Cameras are already flashing through blackened windows and I'm almost convicted when, just in time, I see the wheel bounce in the right-hand lane and roll, not straight ahead, but in a sweetly biased curve, before coming to rest on the verge. It misses everything. No one swerves. No windscreens smash. No cars crash.

I am mighty relieved, need I say, that the force is not with me. How easily I passed by the acts of vandals. How easy, I reflect, to commit one. A sober walker continues on his way, sniffling. The Sporting Arms? Huh!

XV FREE RANGE

It must be relief that makes me greet two teenage girls on the path with a harmless 'Hallo.' They take one look, don't utter a word and hurriedly pass on. I can't imagine that opening my mouth poses a threat and, when I flip my baseball cap round to a law-abiding position, it has absolutely nothing to do with it, or what's gone before. It's the sun moving full frontal.

The heat is reason enough to keep my head down, hug the shade and ease the burning sensation to my ears. A quiet life seems infinitely 'cool'. A whiff of new baked bread from some nearby factory tickles my nose; the very hint I need that it's lunch time.

Beneath some trees, I succumb to two sandwiches (sarnies I was reminded when I bought them yesterday), one cereal bar, two more Pink Ladies and all but the dregs of an orange drink. I remove my boots, peel off the Bart Simpson's, lie back and, when I wake up, an hour has passed of fanciful imaginings in which I've played no part.

I'm into Newburn now and (as if I needed any encouragement) approaching a temptation; the Boathouse, a riverside hostelry. A couple at a picnic table outside are discussing the intricacies of the pub raffle. 'You can win £60,' they tell me, as I perch on the bench-end. 'But if you open the box' (presumably the right one) 'it could be £600.'

They come every week in search of good fortune but I find it on tap, cleaning up on a pint of rough cider before I rejoin the couple. Even the strains of *'Bye Bye Love, Bye Bye Happiness'* from within fail to dispel a certain light-headedness. 'That's a funny dachshund,' I remark to the woman, on observing a slouching canine stretched out below.

'It's a short-legged Jack Russell,' she replies.

'Oh, that explains it then.'

I'm off along the river valley, past families in a riverside park, past sunlight dancing on waters, past the hush of overhanging trees. Even when a powerboat with water-skier in tow disturbs the peace, I find the wake slip-slapping along the shore another reason to give thanks for my new-found freedom.

XVI GIVING BACK

Freedom ... it's written in my stars, I seem to remember. I need to give myself more of it; freedom to drink as much as I like for a start. The orange drink dregs are long since drunk and the rough cider is a nostalgia trip. I've even waved goodbye to my last luscious Pink Lady. Heading up a steep lane away from the river, I'm gasping in this heat. I decide to stop at the next habitation for a fill-up of my plastic bottle.

Asking strangers for a drink of water has always held the happiest of associations, ever since that started a lifelong friendship in my twenties with a couple who lived in an isolated cottage on the edge of a wood. They were the original squatters. Sarge had moved in with his second wife when they found it unoccupied. There was no running water, no mains gas or electricity, no sanitation and no rent. Water was pumped from a spring, cooking was on an old black range, heating was a log fire, washing a jug and bowl of water, bathing a tin bath.

It was primitive and I loved it. It was a taste of how life used to be, when people told stories to the crackle of logs and the flicker of oil lamps. It put me in touch with the pleasures of the past and the redeeming values of hardship, when muscles were built by woodcutting and by grappling with the biggest mugs of tea that ever hands held.

I knock on the first front door, a semi-detached cottage. No answer. And next door. No answer. I go round the back. It's workers' playtime. Everyone's out. But further on, through a courtyard, I spot an open back door to what looks like a mansion. I ring a bell and a clean-cut young man appears on a basement path below.

'Sorry to bother you. But can you manage some water?' I ask, holding up the bottle.

'I launch into a bloodthirsty account of the
Roman emperor, Caracalla.'

'Of course,' he says. 'No trouble. I'll see if I can get some ice in it for you.'

'Brilliant.' And he does.

I find out that this whole complex is a Residential Conference Centre for Newcastle University. He won't accept anything for his trouble, so whether it's the mantle of academia falling round me or the feeling that I ought to give something back, I launch into a bloodthirsty account of the Roman emperor, Caracalla, who arranged for a rival brother to be dispatched in front of their mother and pillaged his way across the Near East. 'But he got his comeuppance. Some malcontent did him in when he dismounted for a quick crap.' I'm not sure he appreciates my 'thank you' gift.

'It's what happens when your back's turned, in't it?' he remarks. 'This Roman stuff is all around and we never have time to mug up on it. It's back to the kitchen for me though.'

Back to reality for me, with the final ascent to Heddon-on-the-Wall, past the homes of retired captains of industry with their Audi A6s, Alfas and Omegas. It's my beginning of the walk along the B6318 or what was the Military Way, shadowing the Wall and originally constructed to permit the rapid movement of troops. At 3.45 p.m., I catch my first sight of anything Roman. It looks suspiciously like a ditch.

XVII ENEMY BEHIND

Knowing where you're going can be a disadvantage. To see ahead, mile after mile, takes away the frisson of unexpectedness that bends hold out. Even ups and downs do nothing to disguise the all-pervasive straightness on this stretch of the Military Way. And, with the sun making a beeline for me from the south-west, my only respite is the shade of an occasional tree on the left of the road.

The Sun God determines everything: day, night, month, year,

even drunken orgies, crawling on pavements and thick ears. But I'm not worshipping; I'll not walk on the right. Walking on the left, though, is heresy. As any walker worth his salt will tell you, walking with traffic behind is not the done thing. The Romans knew it. It's basic army training; always face the enemy. Retribution can be swift and silent. Fast as the road hog comes, I don't hear him until he's right on my back. The sound waves are on his side.

I should know why. You'd hardly credit it, but we have two tellies; one in the lounge and one in the kitchen. When my wife's tuned into the news in the kitchen and I'm doing likewise in the lounge on Sky, all I get is an echo. I might as well be glued to the History Channel.

It's like dinner being served in the dining room, but eaten by someone else by the time I, in the lounge, hear 'It's ready.' It's like getting knocked down before I can wave a white flag. And on this straight stretch there are no cameras or even a legion of Romans in full battledress to arrest the speed merchants. Without a well-cut verge either, most of my walk has to be on the road.

The consequence of all this is that I am getting angry; aerated at having to jump out of my skin without prior notice; alarmed at the thought that, on such a narrow road, a speeding wing mirror could knock me sideways; and finally incandescent to be so hot, bothered and blistered that I'm lurching from side to side anyway. Not only cars but battalions of motorcyclists are doing their ton-ups at the expense of my life expectancy. I'm even more perturbed when I start shaking my fist and shouting 'barbarians' at the top of my voice.

XVIII HOPPING IT

A police bike roars past, siren blaring. This madness has got to stop. Below Harlow Hill, the Roman ditch looks inviting. I find a way in. It's shady. It's cool. And it's not loud. Time to take stock. Mouth parched – the iced drink lasted little longer than the ice; head bashed – the heavy metal is making serious inroads on my sanity; and both feet smarting – another blister has come out in sympathy on my left foot. Not a happy tally, but at least I'm not sniffling. I've sweated out the cold. In fact, there can't be much of me left that's liquid – blood perhaps.

This ditch should be a good spot to stop for a breather but I'm unsettled. A ditch is for things you dispose of and my aggression is still too close. This could have been a last resting place … for barbarians. I imagine they've launched a surprise attack, been repulsed and dived back into the ditch. On the nearside, they crouch for cover but stay a moment too long. The Romans re-arm and pin them down. They're easy prey, trying to escape up the far side. High on the Wall, the Romans dispatch them. Stoned or speared? Not an enviable choice. Is that why the ditch is quiet? I move on.

Luckily, a path parallel to the road takes me forward and, a little further, a friendly tree offers a staging post, a stone at its foot for a seat and a ruffle of leaves for a welcome. This is more like it. I feel we've known each other for years. On again, and in a short while, the only walkers I've seen in miles approach. But their leader looks sombre. 'They're stopping traffic back there. Think a motorcyclist got killed.'

'Little wonder,' I say, shaking my head. 'It'll be a walker next. Take care.'

Then, at 6.20, a sign: hopping across my path, a frog. I notice how still it lies between leaps; how one halt seems to energise it for the next advance. I take my cue. It can't be far. One last spurt – less of a hop, more of a hobble – and at 6.35, ten hours after I started, I make it, my next abode; The Barn, East Wallhouses. It's been a long, long day and Mrs.Walton, I love you.

XIX THE COOLER

Normally, when you meet your landlady, there are hallos, name droppings, room showings, followed by 'what time breakfast?' from the new arrival and 'how do you like your eggs?' from her. Almost the first thing I say, after I ditch the rucksack in the hallway, is 'must take these boots off,' with a few 'phews' when I do. Mrs.W might well add a few 'phews' of her own but, seeing me gingerly test the route to the kitchen, she's good enough not to let on. And when I start prattling on about suicidal maniacs, she takes that in quietly too.

It's not surprising that the conversation turns to the darker side. Mrs.W tells of a relative's experience in Communist-run Poland during the 70s, when the police broke up some rowdy behaviour.

'He made the mistake of answering back. They took him away, stripped him and put him in a cage only this high,' she recounts, making a mark not much above the knee. 'Then a woman hosed cold water on him for an hour. He had a broken nose and bruises all over. The consulate advised him not to go to Eastern Europe ever again.'

'I shouldn't think he'd want to, would he? Not after that.'

Funny how problems with feet can shrink to little toe size. And how relief from my evaporation is threatened by more talk of brutality, as the subject of Saddam Hussein rears its ugly head.

Tell you what,' I interject, trying not to sound terminal. 'You wouldn't happen to have a nice cool drink handy, I suppose?'

'Do you drink baby drinks?' Mrs.W replies. 'I keep them in the fridge for my grandchildren.'

'Absolutely … fine … yes … anything.' I'd put a dummy in my mouth if it was wet.

XX CHANGING TACK

Once creature comforts are catered for, the morrow comes to mind. A not-too-innocent question crops up. 'The Path beyond. By the road, is it?'

'Yes,' Mrs.W informs.

'I suppose some of it's on the road?'

'Up to Chollerford certainly.'

'And how far away would that be?'

'Not sure. A good few miles, maybe ten.'

Pause. I'm thinking tarmac. 'You see, it's my feet.'

'Yes. I guessed.'

'Blisters make it a bit difficult.' Then, a different tack. 'The forecast tomorrow. Have you heard?' I know really, but still ask. 'Hot, is it?'

'Same as today, they say. It might be hotter.'

'Mmm ... thought so.'

Mrs.W is thinking, I can tell, and it's gone quiet in me, a quiet that's full of:

heavy metal thumping,
rucksack humping,
blisters, punctures,
wheels turning,
disasters,
smell of feet burning
and mile upon mile
of plasters.

Mrs.W is a lot faster. 'I know you're walking and perhaps I shouldn't ... but there's a Hopper Bus, you know.'

'A Hopper?' I can't take it in all at once. I should have known, shouldn't I? 'Oh, bus?'

'Yes. There's one tomorrow morning.'

'Really? Sounds like an idea.' I'm toying. 'I suppose I could go a little way ...'

'I'll look up the times.'

' ... until the Path leaves the road, I mean ... at Chollerford, you say?'

'Round about, yes.'

'There. At 9.52 it stops at Heddon-on-the-Wall. Should be here soon after. You'll catch it at 10.'

'Chollerford … umm. Look … Housesteads isn't far beyond. That's the fort I really want to see.'

'It stops there too.'

'That's where I'll go then. Well, that's a relief.'

'And breakfast?'

'Nine o'clock will be fine.'

'Eggs?'

'Yes.'

'How do you like them?'

'Oh … scrambled please.'

Footnote: There is now off-road provision for walkers over this section of Hadrian's Wall Path.

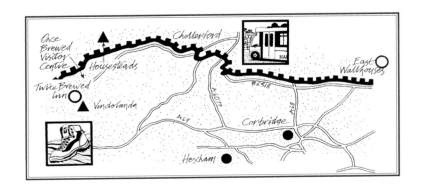

DAY TWO

'What puts me most in touch with the men who manned these walls ... is a game.'

XXI CUTTING CORNERS

I wake, fresh from witnessing a miraculous escape: in my dream a plane flies past, right outside my window. 'It's going to crash,' I cry out. It's on fire. It has crashed, round a corner. I get up. I run. Better help ... quick. But when I turn the corner, what do I see? A burnt-out bus instead. And the passengers? They're safe in a shed alongside.

Oh, that's all right then. The bus it is.

Now dreams are very well, but what amazes me is that, after only one day's walking, without anything you could call heart-searching, I have jettisoned my plan to walk the whole of Hadrian's Wall Path. That's what I told people I'm going to do. They're expecting me to do it. I'm expecting me to do it. Seriously, do a couple of blisters, a very hot day and mad blighters doing ton-ups on a Roman road justify my changing horses, just like that? Shanks's pony one moment ... Hopalong Express the next. Very convenient, I'm sure. But convenience isn't ... wasn't my bag. This is a personal challenge I'm on, for God's sake.

What about those intrepid walkers who pull sledges hundreds of miles across the Arctic wastes to the North Pole, braving ice floes, jagged ice fields, polar bears' teeth and a wind chill factor so many degrees below that it'll freeze your pee and send it back to you before you've finished? Do they hop on the first light plane when they run out of Milky Bars? Of course not. Or only in commercials. 'I got a quarter of the way in one day with blisters,' I might mutter but that doesn't cut any ice. And 'I had a dream' simply doesn't ring true when it lets you off the hook.

So, when I board the Hopper Bus (otherwise called Hadrian's Wall Bus AD 122, the year construction started) and the man in front turns round, saying 'I'm Paul, your Personal Tour Guide,' and the tour is of places that, if I intended to see, it wouldn't be this way, thank you, might I be forgiven for muttering 'really' with underwhelming enthusiasm? While he's telling me about the oldest jail in England at Hexham or the bread-oven built into a church wall to make sure local people paid their tax on dough, my attention is wandering, much like my feet should be. I'm more entertained by the lady behind who informs me it costs £25 for a blow-dry here, when it's only £8.50 at Wallsend.

I do pick up one piece of priceless information, though. There are very few B & B places at Bowness-on-Solway. Paul says The Kings Arms is good, but urges me to try and book it through the Once Brewed Visitor Centre further on. I'll be lucky to get in, it seems. But Bowness is the end of my walk. This isn't. I have to come back to the present. I'm not giving up, am I? This is just a hiccup. What was that bit in my stars? From Sunday, it said, the Full Moon gives me that extra determination. It's Monday today. Yes, I *am* determined. I may be on the bus now but, when I get to Housesteads, mark my words: I'm going to walk again.

XXII ROLE PLAY

It's eleven o'clock and I've arrived. Housesteads is huge and I'm humbled. As a walker, I should have been glimpsing it from afar, enthralled by its escarpment setting. If I had approached from the Path, I would have been grasping the significance of its scale and layout, bit by bit. But spewed out from the bus, I'm not ready to take it in. It's all too sudden, like a present opened before a birthday.

Besides, I have this identity crisis. Who am I? A drop-in tourist or dropout walker? The visitor centre buys me time and I buy a decent map; the Hadrian's Wall Path map. Why on earth didn't I do so before? It's packed with useful information – like how to get where you're going, would you believe – and what to see on the way. And now there are all these display cases, loaded with artefacts and figures, I can bury my head in them.

Housesteads is only one of sixteen forts that serviced Hadrian's Wall, but what survives makes it the most complete Roman fort in northern Europe. It was not just a garrison, but virtually a small town, being home to about 1000 soldiers. Here were all the facilities they would have needed; barracks and stables, of course, but granaries, hospital, chapel and workshops too. The latrine block is the finest example of such in Britain. There are also remains of a civilian settlement (*vicus*) that sprang up outside the fort walls.

I mug up on the Wall itself. Up to 15 feet high and 10 feet high, it stretched 73 English miles, built of stone for the greater part of its length. On either side ran a ditch, the southern one called the *vallum*, some 9 feet deep. Construction took place between AD 122 and 130. Every Roman mile (1000 paces or 1480 metres), a fortified milecastle was built functioning as a guard post. Between each milecastle at specific distances, there were two watchtower turrets. All this was across terrain that any civil engineering firm would find demanding. Altogether it was an immense undertaking that marked the northern frontier of the Roman Empire for some 300 years and makes Hadrian's Wall today a World Heritage Site.

Yet, impressive as this achievement is, my attention is grabbed by one display cabinet, the contents of which are devoted to a game. It's the name that grips me; *Ludus latrunculorum*. It keeps tripping off my tongue. It's the best play on words yet. I can imagine men saying, 'Come on, chaps. Who's *for ... um latrunculorum?*' Lots of them, I bet. It was the Soldier's Game. The board, made of sandstone, was divided into squares (nine x five) by incised lines and the game played with counters improvised from stone, glass or shards of pottery. The aim was to capture all enemy pieces by trapping them between one's own. And when you did, you were proclaimed *Imperator*: Emperor. I'm transported back to boyhood. Jumping on some hillock, I can hear myself taunting my sister with, 'I'm the king of the castle. You're the dirty rascal.'

Walls rise and fall. Empires come and go. What don't change are raw human emotions. The will to win is high among them, the thrill of victory universal. Strange that what puts me most in touch with the men who manned these walls some 1800 years ago is a game.

XXIII RULE CHANGE

More in tune now, I'm ready to explore the fort. A short climb and I reach the perimeter. Instead of going in though, I patrol the outside. Soon I come across the remains of the traders' settlement. Here was a tavern, not large – I pace it out – about 18 yards x 8 yards. I conjure up the crowd; the bustle, shouts of greeting, the jostling for attention from off-duty soldiers and the raucous laughter, friendly banter or fierce arguments after a few drinks. Sobering up, I see to the right a so-called 'murder house' where two skeletons were found; one a woman, the other a middle-aged man with a knife point wedged between his ribs. What was it, I wonder? A broken promise, unpaid debt, a trust betrayed?

Men trained for battle can never be far from a fight, if only in mind. But I don't need telling that the Romans were far more than a fighting machine. My first close-up of Hadrian's Wall at 11.50 is eloquent enough. I see how accurately the stone is cut and dressed, how true the courses run, even up the steepest incline. From large-scale plan down to working detail, here is the evidence of well-ordered minds and finely-honed skills. With one stroke of my hand across the surface, I pass my admiration down the ages.

Then, as I limp down to a gateway – the Knag Burn gateway – an oldish couple gain ground on me.

'No fools wor they,' the man says. 'See those walls. Only legionaries built 'em. Didn't trust auxiliaries, did they. Nah. It's them who had to dig ditches.'

'Oh, I see.'

He has the no-nonsense speech of a Yorkshireman. His wife lets him do all the talking. 'Ah, but them Romans weren't what they wor cracked up to be. Credit to barbarians, they wor a canny crew. Up they'd come, pick a fight, inflict casualties, get knocked abaht p'raps. But when chips wor down and they looked like losing, they'd scarper, melt into night. Them Romans only knew to stand and fight. Score in set-piece battle, they would, but couldn't cope with skirmish.'

'Well, that's rich, isn't it, fighting force that they were.'

I spend a little more time wandering round the remains. Each of the barracks was neatly divided into ten rooms, to accommodate 80 men, with larger quarters for the centurions at the far end. At first I think the granaries are bathhouses, with rows of pillared supports as with a hypocaust system, until I read that these bore joists, so that stores could be ventilated and vermin deterred.

But all the time, the Yorkshireman's words are nagging away at me; 'They couldn't cope with that.' No, of course not. I realise why they've registered with me. The Romans were too inflexible, too tied to a strategy. You have to adapt. That's what I've done, isn't it? I've adapted. I've had to. My game's changed.

Thanks to my visit to Housesteads, I feel a new enthusiasm breaking out. The Path continues through woodland, and the only section where you can actually walk on the Wall. At 12.50, I step out, best foot forward – the best one I can find anyway.

XXIV PASSING TIME

It's good to be walking again and, with a light breeze, cooler. Walking in woodland, five feet or so above ground level, is – well – elevating, if semi-detached. Above me are Scots pine and sycamore, below foxgloves and bracken. On both sides, the landscape stretches for miles, Scotland to the north, Pennines to the south.

Fresh from Housesteads though, I'm caught in the past. I imagine this wall fifteen feet high, in full view of the surrounding terrain. How would I have felt then? In command, yes, but a remote sort of control; secure enough atop all the masonry, but bored, and perhaps a touch complacent after weeks of inaction. Up here, I'd be unassailable by day but by night, what then? Ought I to be more vigilant? Was that a rustle of wind or men snaking through grass?

What if I were one of those manning the Knag Burn gateway

down in the valley? Might that hoot of an owl be a call to attack? How easy for a trader, passing through by day, to wise up on the changes of watch as he begrudgingly pays his dues.

'How long before your next swig of beer, good soldier?' he might ask.

'Oh, another three hours yet.'

'Thar's a pity, or you could join us in a jar,' he banters.

'That's enough, fellow. On your way now.'

And off the trader goes, armed with the knowledge of when the watch changes and able to calculate the best time for his mates to mount an assault. Not much different from casually revealing holiday plans to some stranger, only to find one's home burgled on return.

Preoccupied as I am with these speculations, I hardly notice the jerky gait I've adopted to ease the smarting of the blister on the heel of my right foot and on the ball of the other. Before I realise it, I'm off the Wall, walking alongside it, a companion that's going to be with me for many a mile, raising questions that won't go away.

XXV STEPPING BACK

The first question is: how is it that a Wall fifteen feet high reduces uniformly to about five feet? Obviously, 1800 years or so take their toll. Walls crumble and fall, but who's been tidying up and how? That brings me to question two: how come the Wall looks dry-stone built? Surely it would take more than that to withstand this punishing environment.

Question three, though, is the one that bugs me: why are there dog-legs every so often? Those step-backs in the line of the Wall must be out of character. Weren't Romans obsessed with straightness? Such is *my* obsession that I quiz walking-parties on the way. 'Haven't seen them'; 'What d'you mean?'; 'Where?' are typical responses. It beats me how they can walk for miles and not even see staggers. Staggering is all I see.

I argue my case with one chap. 'Romans never do anything without reason.'

'Except Italians,' he retorts.

I'm looking for a sensible answer. A clue would do. At last, I find a man who's seen, a scholar indeed, keen to add to the sum of human knowledge.

'Did you notice the dog-legs are closed off?' he prompts. He means that the end of one stone meets the side of another, making a strong bond. Well, no, I didn't. But that would add weight to *hypothesis one*: that the dog-legs provide the extra support a high dry-stone wall would need.

But, by this time, I am busy processing *hypothesis two*: that the dog-legs are distance markers. My test is simple enough – pacing the distance between dog-legs. I start from the dog-leg just passed. 50 paces it is to the next, 163 paces to the one after, then 49, 154 and finally 101, before the Wall narrows too much for a dog-leg to get a look-in. I'm looking for consistency. I haven't found it, though I observe the numbers are rough multiples of 50, *very* rough. I could put the discrepancies down to my staggering.

Instead, I abandon all pretence and go for broke with *hypothesis three*: marking time. When the legionaries built the wall, they did so in gangs, no doubt, each allocated a certain time before the next gang took over. If so, they or their centurion would surely have to account for the work completed. The dog-leg would do it, the step back marking each stretch. What's more, the chief engineer could take the credit for raising the competitive spirit. And so on, up the line. That being the case, what would the 49 pacers say to the 163 aces? Something like, 'Ran out of stone, didn't we? It's them who couldn't keep up.' Blame always goes down the line, naturally. Or, 'Yeah, and who didn't have to fight off 200 barbarians?'

One woman came up with a more plausible explanation for the variations. 'You wouldn't want to be building that in the height of winter, would you? Just imagine the winds, the rain and the cold. They must have been real toughies.' Some more affected than others, certainly.

　　　　　　　　　　[DAY TWO]

XXVI THE HUMP

A nd that's what gets me, when I see two thirty-something women in shorts striking out manfully towards a steep hump (crag in the vernacular) that this switchback section has thrown up. The Wall follows it like the spine of some angry dragon but they seem determined to follow the most spiteful route. Goaded to action, I speed up to intercept them before their ascent.

'Excuse me. Taking the high road, are you?'

'Yup,' the taller one answers brusquely, without stopping. 'We're in for the challenge.'

This is a bit of a put-down but I don't rise to the bait. Instead, I continue skirting the outcrop, away from the line of the Wall, all the time in heated discussion … with myself. Hell-bent on one thing, aren't they: getting there. They can't have blisters, can they? Why not? Good to have an aim though. But, stumping on like that, despite everything, what are they missing?

Did they stop to take in that daunting rampart of a cliff face, topped by the Wall and with a sheer drop to Crag Lough, the lake at its foot? Were they impressed by the commanding view of the landscape beyond, dotted with clumps of trees?

One hiker I met likened the trees to a group of borderers mustering forces before an attack. He'd let his imagination off the leash. Had they given themselves the chance to get the feel of the place and notice things?

Noticing things? That gives me an idea. As I round the bend, I see them coming over the top. If I move up a gear, I'll catch them coming down the other side. I feel like holding them up. Awful, isn't it.

'Oh, hallo again. Tell you what,' I say, 'you didn't happen to spot those dog-legs in the Wall, did you?' They look at me like I cocked one up.

'No. Not at all.'

There I am, vindicated. They're not interested. Not one bit. No follow-up question. Probably wouldn't know what a dog-

*'… that daunting rampart of a cliff face, topped by
the Wall and with a sheer drop to Crag Lough …'*

leg was if they saw it. Don't even want to admit it. With that, they stamp the ground like wild horses and stick their noses in the air before snorting off, deep in a conversation that I'd hardly interrupted. I just catch the tail-end of a sentence. It's something like, 'Compared with the rest of them, Adrian is good for his age.' There you have it … teachers. They might be getting a move on, but they haven't left school yet. They're still in the classroom. I don't feel so bad after all.

I was going to ask them about blisters; how they avoid getting them and what they'd do if they did. But no hope, nope. The professional talkers are already galloping away with the answers, leaving me to my own dialogue. Walking alone as I am, I'm learning. Not slavishly following anyone or anything, I'm able to take things in as I go along, watching, waiting sometimes, playing with opportunities. I'm open to new experience. 'Yes, I know,' my alter ego butts in,' but don't you think, with your baseball cap back to front again, you looked a bit of a Charlie?'

XXVII SHEEPISH LOOKS

Well, possibly, I answer but how would I know? I can't see myself as others see me. Nor can they. We see others only from where we are, coloured by opinions we trundle out like overloaded shopping trolleys. And I suppose it's as crass of me to criticise their single-mindedness as it might be of them to give my baseball cap short shrift.

But, methinks, one thinks too much. I turn to a black-headed sheep for relief. With the thickest pile of wool I've seen on any carpet, it's lolling on its side in full sun. No worries. Oblivious. But his mate's on the lookout. One glance at me and she legs it. And then, so does he. Am I *that* threatening?

Out of interest, I pace the distance and reckon ten yards is the closest she let me get. Having nothing better to do, I extend the research project. I'm pleased to report that the next sheep finds me more approachable. I'm only seven and a half yards away before it takes flight, though in fairness, it was preoccupied with a tasty patch of grass.

Nothing like food to take one's mind off. Which reminds me … it's 2.40 p.m. and high time I get close to a spot of lunch. It's Chicken Tikka Masala – wonderful what meals you find in a crisp packet. Then, straight to dessert, a Cadbury brunch bar, before my eyes settle on that Northumberland fruit cake. Its place in history has to be settled now. The spoils of victory are not easily won. It takes a scissor point to gain entry to Colin's well-wrapped package, but the effort is rewarded. This is the main course.

While I'm tucking in, a party of hikers going the other way stop for a chat.

'Where did you start?' I ask.

'Bowness,' one says, 'and I must tell you we had a superb meal at The Kings Arms. Only £25 for the four of us.'

'No,' I say, taken aback not so much by the value as the name. 'That's the place I was told I had to book … at the Once Brewed Visitor Centre. Hope I get in.' There's a purpose in my stride as I set off. Single-minded, one might say.

XXVIII NAME CALLING

'We knew you were coming,' they say, when I ask at the Visitor Centre about booking The Kings Arms. I am blown away.

'What? How?' I stammer. 'You know?'

'Yes. Paul told us.'

'Paul who? Aah.' I begin to touch down. 'You mean Paul on the Hopper bus, do you?'

'Yes. He called in, told us to expect you and to see what we could do.'

But then, how did he know my name? Got it … that visitor questionnaire he asked me to fill in on the bus. I signed it. 'How terribly kind of him.'

One injection of thoughtfulness and I'm suffering from an overdose of optimism. So when the lady at the desk phones The Kings Arms, tells me that they do have a spare room and that they've booked me in for Friday night, I'm expecting even more good news: like the answer to one pressing question, and not about the Wall.

'Can you explain something?'

'I'll do my best,' she says.

'Well, you're the Once Brewed Centre and I'm staying at the Twice Brewed Inn tonight. Must be a story there. Is it about beer or tea?'

'It's both.'

The answer is soaked in history, bringing in the Jacobite rebellion and Bonnie Prince Charlie amongst others. It goes something like this; a road had to be built between Newcastle and Carlisle, so that any future Pretender to the throne could be chased and caught, the first one having escaped. In 1751, the builders being tired and thirsty (or just being builders) stopped at this inn, which is about half-way, for a pint of the local tipple. But they found it so weak-kneed that they insisted it be brewed again. Hence the Twice Brewed Inn.

When, in 1934, the Youth Hostel was built nearby, the teetotaller Lady Trevelyan made the opening speech. Referring to the pub, she said that, of course, no alcohol would be served at the hostel and she hoped the tea and coffee would be brewed only once. Later still, the Visitor Centre (the Northumberland National Park Centre) took its name from the hostel. It's all very neat.

But the lady saves the greatest relish for a small aside. 'You know the Geordies are so called from supporting King George against the Pretender,' she informs me, straight-faced. 'What a good job there wasn't a King William on the throne at the time, or just think what they'd be called.'

But it's down to serious business now: the Wall.

XXIX WALL MATTERS

'You'd better speak to someone who knows.' She directs me to a chap in the corner arranging a display.

'It's about the Wall … a few queries … wondered if you could help?'

'Sure.'

'The height for a start. It was up to fifteen feet high, I know, but it looks as though the remains have been tidied up. A lot of that last section is very level.'

'Yes, of course. The Victorians rebuilt much of it, but only so high.'

'And it's dry-stone. Is that right?'

'That's how they rebuilt it, capping with turf. The original Wall was of dressed sandstone and wider. The other local stone which can't be dressed (Whinstone, we call it) was used for infill. And the Romans did use mortar, made from crushed limestone, mixed with oil. They reckon up to 75% oil. That was why it lasted so well, except that much of the stone was pilfered and re-cycled. You'll see it in other buildings along the way.'

'Opportunists took advantage, I suppose. I'll look out for that. One thing which made me curious is; have you any idea why there's a dog-leg in the Wall every so often? Could the Victorians have put them in (*hypothesis four*) or would they have followed the Roman practice?'

'Can't say for sure, but the Romans built the Wall in separate sections, some thicker than others. It wasn't one continuous run, so they'd have to join up somehow where the sections met.' Well, there's *hypothesis five* for you.

'I wondered if the dog-legs were markers to show how far they'd got?'

'Could have been. Many sections had a stone built into the Wall, with the name of the centurion responsible carved on it.'

'They wanted their work recognised.'

'Yes. Some of those stones survive. But as to the dog-legs, no

47

one really knows.'

'I see. Well, many thanks.'

He was a gold mine of information. I'm sure you can read up about this but there's nothing to beat hearing it first-hand. I liked the centurion's name being carved. Wouldn't we all want to leave some permanent mark?

The funny fact is that I'm most heartened by the one question he couldn't answer; about the dog-legs. I wonder too how much of the original Wall remains as the Romans built it and how much has been reconstructed. But that's all to the good. When there's still more to find out, there's every reason to carry on asking. Sometimes, it's good to be uncertain.

XXX UNCOMMON SENSE

It's time to check in at 'Twice Brewed'. I've drawn room 17. It's a bit small and there's no view but I'm not complaining. I'm certainly not in a going-to-get-this-pub-renamed-if-it's-the-last-thing-I-do mood. Except for one thing: in the corner, there is a suitcase. Its label identifies the owner as Alison Brown.

'Excuse me.' I'm down at the bar. 'I believe someone's already in 17, or their suitcase is. Trouble is we might not get on but, who knows? It might be worth a try.'

The bar girl is used to ribaldry, I can tell. She ignores my nonsense and shouts out to the landlady, 'Pauline, we've double booked 17. Can we do 6 instead? It's a twin.' Everything's done in twos at Twice Brewed.

'Yes. That's all right.'

Brilliant. So I head upstairs again, past the clock that goes backwards and one of those hopelessly-grinning faces that hardly needs the caption, 'If you look like this, you probably shouldn't have another one'. After I see room 6, I'm grinning without a first one. It's a good size. It's bright and has a clear view right up to Winshields Crags on Whin Sill ridge. Perfect.

Satisfying my thirst with a modest lemonade and lime, I start to walk the short distance – over a mile – to Vindolanda, another of the must-see sites on my hit list. I'm in an uncommonly buoyant frame of mind. I've acquired an even-when-things-go-wrong-it-comes-right belief system, making me so in tune with my surroundings that the whole world seems to be rooting for me. So much so that, when the brakes squeal three times on an HGV, they sound solicitous. I'm utterly convinced they are articulating, 'How are you?' and, even as I hobble towards my destination, I have no hesitation in yelling back, 'Me? I'm bloody great.'

XXXI HUMAN FACES

If Housesteads is imposing in its hillside setting, Vindolanda, cradled in and around a valley, is engaging. Where Housesteads commands, Vindolanda conjures up a pastoral prospect. I am made welcome from the start. Since time is short, it's suggested I visit the museum first, then look round outside before letting myself out after closing time. How about that? One circuit of the museum and one conclusion: for an insight into the everyday lives of Roman people, this has to be the place.

In my teens, I found a collection of early twentieth century postcards in a junk shop, written by a mother from abroad to her two young sons. She wished Roger a happy birthday, Humphrey a quick recovery from chicken pox, and suchlike. Nothing extraordinary, but I still have those postcards and the unanswered question of why she left her sons behind. That was 100 years ago.

At Vindolanda, you can peruse what people wrote eighteen centuries ago. Thanks to favourable soil conditions, the commitment of the Birley family and some conservation wizardry, over 1900 writing tablets survive to tell the tale of what life was like. Not just for high-ups, but the common soldier: his words are here too.

So what were the matters of moment? In the very first tablet discovered, someone says he is sending socks, sandals and underpants. Bet they were appreciated. On one tablet, a pair of shears is requested. Another relates that beer supplies are low. Claudia Severa's tablet invites a friend, Sulpicia Lepidina, to her birthday on September 11th. How did it go? Much wine, for sure, and perhaps a rendition of 'happy birthday' but dear Claudia could never have known how memorable her invitation would become.

There is nothing so extraordinary about these notes as their very ordinariness. They put a human face on history that the best preserved buildings never can. They show real people with preoccupations I can identify with, underpants and all. The discovery of these tablets was reported all over the world, from the China Daily to the Chicago Tribune, yet how many of us know about them?

There are displays of countless finds. I'm on information overload. The oddest items grab me. Apparently, the women wore wigs made of locally-grown hair moss, especially good at fending off locally-grown midges. I can't imagine which was worse. The footwear catches my eye. I could do with a *caliga*. The open-work uppers are exactly what my feet need, right now.

But one fact stands out. Taken from the average ages on tombstones, life expectancy for men was 40 and for women 28. What a different perspective that would put on things. It's OK for me, with my it-all-comes-right-in-the-end belief but, if it were curtains at 40, I wouldn't be around to believe it. And what about women? If they only lived to 28, they'd hardly see children into their teens. That is separation.

XXXII SILENT VOICES

I'm not surprised the Romans turned to the spirit world. As I enter a temple reconstruction, a bell tings. 'Hear my prayer. I bring offerings of fruit and bread. Please protect my son, Marcus Octavius, on his long journey.' Other pleas are for forgiveness, good health and, more critically, respite from rainfall. 'Vent not your fury on us.' We know that feeling. The gods have a lot to answer for but what gods inflict gods can take away ... my feet for a start. Or at least the smarting. That's my petition.

I've walked the Roman road, seen the bathhouse stokehole, visited the Roman shop, climbed the replica turret, peered down on excavations and now I'm sitting on a bench. Boots off, it's heaven. Everyone has left; the staff, visitors and populace of this settlement before them ... all gone. I'm alone, one still figure in what was a thriving community. The only sound to break through the wind that rustles this valley is the caw of a crow, haunting the ages. But for my breathing, I might almost not be here.

What of the sounds that once sliced this air? The chatter that went with the daily round of waking, eating, working, with perhaps some gaming or bathing before retiring to bed. Do I hear tired footfalls after a day's work? I'd like to. The shadows of those people can't be far from crossing mine. And what of wants and wishes, hopes and fears? We have their words. To be party to their passions and pains, that would be something else. Letters may be written on tablets, but not loves, not tears.

I let myself out and start trudging back to the Twice Brewed when, at 8 p.m., I stumble across a mole – the first mole I've ever seen in the flesh, but dead. Yesterday, explorer; today, run over. Then, who do I see walking towards me but the scholarly man who noticed the dog-leg in the Wall?

'We meet again,' I say. It's a brush with a more recent past.

'There's so much to learn,' he tells me. 'I met a German who came for two to three days last year. This time he's staying eleven days, studying. I'll be coming back tomorrow. And you?'

'Me? I have to travel on.'

Walking always leads one on. In a car, you have to know where you're going, you meet no one and, when you get there, you've gone. On foot, if you let go there's no knowing what you may discover, whose path you may cross or what change that might make in where you'll be. And Mr.Mole, I'm afraid it's too late to warn you just how unpredictable not knowing is.

XXXIII CASE NOTES

Back at Twice Brewed, the peppered, smoked mackerel goes down a treat, and no complaints about the beer. I'm about to open a book I bought at Vindolanda when I notice a change in the ambience. A woman sits close by, with a drink. She could have sat further away. Maybe she's leaving room for a companion on the other side.

I start reading about Roman soldiers. However interesting life in a fort might be, life much closer is occupying me. It's just entered my head … I'm contemplating the possibility that she might happen to answer to the name of Alison. Does she look like an Alison? How does an Alison look? It's not easy to judge sideways.

Minutes have gone by. No one else has arrived, nor is she looking round. She seems content to sit next to her drink and, not to put too fine a point on it … me. The soldiers are on the march. What does it take to open up a conversation? In a word; the question of whether you might have shared a bedroom with the woman sitting right next to you, who doesn't even know it. But I can't jump straight in.

'Excellent meals here.'

'Aren't they.' In her thirties I'd say, middleish.

'You waiting then?'

'No. I've eaten thanks.' Then I see the boots.

'You're walking?'

'Yes. From Carlisle.'

'That's where I'm heading. How are you making out?'

'Fine. How about you?'

'OK, but the road section hammered my feet.'

'Talking about blisters are you?'

'Afraid so.'

'You know the treatment?' With hair clipped up at the back, she has authority.

'I've been wondering.'

'Tell you what I've found best … talcum powder.'

'I'd never have thought, but yes … '

'Feet sweat, especially this weather. Humidity gets trapped. That does it. I just sprinkle the talc inside the socks. Keeps my feet dry and stops the chafing. Simple.'

'I like that, but I've got them already … blisters. Two days now and it's telling.'

'You have? OK. You know what?'

'What?'

'You've got to puncture them.'

A wince. 'Puncture?'

'Of course, you wouldn't if it was a burn blister, but a friction blister, yes.'

'I have to do that, do I?'

'You must burst them. They've got to be dry.'

'I see.'

'And then cut away as much of the skin as you can.'

'No. Gosh. Really?'

'Yes.'

I'm not sure I want to hear this. The punishment sounds worse than the crime. But, if that's what it takes. 'Just one thing; where can I get talc round here?'

'No problem. I've got some I can let you have.'

'That's very kind. Thanks.'

XXXIV CHOICE QUESTIONS

'Obvious, when you think about it – the treatment, I mean.' 'It's like that. When you're too close to something, it often needs someone else to see it. But try telling most people what's best for them and they won't listen.'

'Understandable, I suppose. We only hear what we want to, like plugging our ears into the same old tape.'

'It's the choices people make and how. Listen to this.' She holds out a hand, fingers and thumb pinched. 'Here's a mint choc chip ice. Do you want it? What do you say?'

'I'll say, yes please.'

'But you say yes because … well … the only other choice is no, which you might have said if you couldn't stand chocolate or mint.'

'True. But I like mint chocolate.'

'OK, but how about if I say instead, which would you like – vanilla or strawberry?'

'I'd go for vanilla. Strawberry's too sweet.'

'There you are. The choice is two yeses, not yes or no. That's the point. Too many see only black or white.'

'Yes. But what if the choice is yes or no?'

'How do you mean?'

'Say in a relationship. You know, when it comes to, "you stay, I leave".'

'It depends. There are ways of dealing with it.'

'Such as …'

She sighs. 'I could have divorced my husband. He's terrible with money. Never pays bills. We've been close to the bailiffs several times. It drives me mad. But he's a great chap and I love him.'

'So how do you handle it?'

'Accept him. It's saying yes. What you do is grant people the freedom to be who they are.'

'That doesn't help *you* much though.'

'Not straight away perhaps. But, if I accept him as he is, he'll be more willing to change. It's the best hope.'

'My Dad never would change. Only three when his parents died, both of them, and such cruelty in an orphanage: cold baths and toenails cut till it drew blood. He couldn't trust anyone after that, so what did he do? Became a copper.'

'I know. It's not easy with that sort of background. But there's always some choice. You can choose to move on. You can't stand still.'

'No, that's true. His salvation was the trombone. That pulled his life round. One lucky break can make all the difference.'

'Oh, I know.'

'It's how you are, isn't it, that makes things happen the way they do?' I tell her about finding fivers when you're happy. 'Not that I did.'

'Stop there,' she says. 'I must hear this.' And she rushes off. The loo, I guess. And I'm left wondering what I'm going to say that she must hear.

XXXV HAPPY RETURNS

I'm off on the fiver thing, so when she comes back, all I can think of is that I found the Path, not the fiver.

'That's it,' she says emphatically. 'You look for one thing, something you think you want, but find something else. And that might be just what you need.'

'Or, when you really need something, it finds you ... like the rolls of plaster I found in a market. They've kept me going this far.'

'Yes. You've got to keep an open mind, that's the key. It works this way too; my next door neighbour was moving to Gambia – big life-change. She needed help to clear her house. Desperate, she was. So I dropped everything, spent a lot of time shifting and packing her stuff. But it'll come back. It always does ... some other way perhaps.'

'You make it sound automatic.'

'It's like money in the bank. You credit someone else's account with a favour but you've earned a credit in yours that you draw on later. I have remarkable friends. I could phone them up out of the blue and say "turn up at Carlisle tomorrow with a trailer and £500". No reason given but they'll be there. They'll do it. They know it works.'

'Amazing. We think too much, don't we, and stop things happening.'

'Yes. You have to be spontaneous. You're worth a rise? Ask for it. Takes courage, but you've lost nothing and, who knows, you might get a bigger mileage allowance? Act on your gut feelings.

I do. I have this old aunt and uncle, lovely couple. I was away, thinking about them, so I picked up the phone to let them know how much I loved them.'

'That's touching. It's things which stare us in the face, that we don't do and wish we had when we find out why. There've been times I wish I'd acted …'

'Sure. Hey, look I have to go now. Great, talking.'

'Yes, it was. Oh … you said about the talc.'

'I hadn't forgotten. It's back at the hostel.'

'Aah … the youth hostel. That's where you're staying? I see.'

'OK, I'll meet you with it, in the car park tomorrow. Nine o'clock. All right?'

'Yes. Fine.'

I'm back in my room. So she's not Alison after all. I should have guessed. It's obvious now. What walker would ever have a suitcase? Yet, if I hadn't seen the suitcase, would we even have spoken? I don't know. And, with all that talk, I feel as though I've stuffed myself. It was eat-as-much-as-you-like: be spontaneous … play your luck … say yes … accept, if you'd like someone to change … act, if you want to change… look for one thing, find another … and happy returns when you've done a good turn.

It's a lot to take in. It's like five portions of fruit or veg a day? So obviously good for you that you never get around to doing it. I've had tastes but this is more. And when someone like – good heavens, I still don't know her name – speaks from experience that clinches it. It's not just where I've been or where I'm going. It's where I want to go. But, before I get completely carried away, there is the tiny matter of the feet.

XXXVI THE SURGERY

Burst them? The only spike I possess is one safety pin (wisely included by my dear wife, presumably on the basis that, if all else fails, at least I keep my trousers up). I sit on the bed, hoist right leg over left knee and gently peel off the plaster that's strapping the heel. Quite unprepared, never having popped a blister in my life, I jab the point in. I see what the Alison-type person means about keeping it dry. I'm shocked to see droplets of a clear-looking fluid drip on to the carpet; for the carpet and for me. Sixty per cent water, aren't we? There's plenty left. Enlightened somewhat, I attend to the other blister which now discharges its cargo on to a strategically placed tissue.

This is like being prepped for an operation. But make no mistake, cutting is what it's about. You can rationalise; it's dead skin isn't it, but cutting bits off is not slicing an onion. It's myself I'll be getting rid of.

Having nothing better to do, I've entertained myself at odd times (very odd times) rubbing my beard vigorously and being mildly amused at the sprinkling of fine powder that descends. Look, there I am, I say; a pile of dust. Look at me now. I am about to add to my remains and armed only with the smallest of scissors. The forced entry to Colin's Northumberland fruit cake was a doddle set against this surgical operation.

The first blister having been punctured, it's lying low and not easy to find a way in. I have to lift it again. With the safety pin point in my right hand, I prod the puncture hole and prise up the blister into a reasonable dome shape, leaving my left hand (gammy-handed as I am) free to snip just below it.

This is all very well toward the centre of the dome but there are problems:

1. I need to cut round the back of the puncture hole to complete the circle, while I'm still holding it up. But then (a) I'd lose my purchase point and (b) I can't.
2. When I try to cut away to the edge of the dome (a) I have to lift the dome higher to see what I'm doing and (b) it hurts.
3. Pulling up the dead skin tugs on what's still alive so (a) I won't and (b) I don't.

I settle for a blister with jabs in.

Cutting the blister on the left foot is more problematical. I go through the motions: left foot over right; scissors in left hand ready to cut; safety pin in right hand ready to prise up. Prise up. But this blister is on the ball of the foot and I can't reach forward enough to get my left hand anywhere near enough to do the cutting. Besides, the angles are all obtuse. Short of combining a degree in contortionism with a black belt in Ju-Jitsu, there is no way this surgery can proceed. I settle for the puncture on this foot. It's a truce. I'll live with dead skin. Without, I won't.

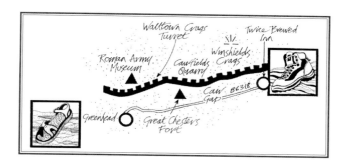

DAY THREE

'The purpose is in the playing. The challenge is how.'

XXXVII WILD POPPIES

In the car park, on the dot, she hands me this neatly prepared packet.

'I feel like a drug-pusher,' she smiles. 'Instructions inside. How did you get on?'

'Well and truly punctured, I'd say,' I say, keeping quiet about the unfinished business. Thank goodness, she doesn't mention the cut.

'Good. You'll make it now. No trouble.'

'I'm sure, thanks to you.'

'Good luck then.'

'You too. Oh, I forgot to ask your name.'

'Sue.'

'And I'm Laurence. Thanks for everything; talc and the talk. I won't forget that in a hurry.'

'Great to meet you. Have a marvellous walk.'

Opening the packet back in my room, I find more than I bargained for; not just a sachet of talc but a sweet (how sweet) and a note. The instructions are not what I'd expected: '*On the last hill, sing "Over the Rainbow" and melt the enclosed lemon drop along with your troubles. Have fun. Sue.*' That stops me. What last hill is she talking about?

And the song? A bit schmaltzy perhaps, but what the heck. It's a nice idea. It sets me off on a sentimental journey that includes, '*The hills are alive with the ...*' (heaven forbid), '*Pack up your troubles*', before moving quickly on to the only song I can ever remember the words of, the hippopotamus song. '*Mud, mud, glorious mud*' was a favourite refrain on caving expeditions in my twenties. I allow myself a fond reprise of Jim Langham's backside stuck firmly in a tight hole at the top of a twelve foot climb, with me behind wondering how to get out. Then I'm back at '*The Rainbow*', drawing a blank on all but the first line. Still, in my positive thinking mind, I know I can rustle up something when the time comes.

It's 10.20 a.m. when I set off. I'm well fed with great scrambled eggs, fluffy as they come and Twice Brewed knocked me up a last-minute packed lunch. I'm showered, shaved and spruced up to the nines. And boy, do I smell good. I'm talcumed well enough to meet my maker – feet first.

I may be nearly halfway to my destination, Bowness, but I feel as though I'm starting afresh. It's not so much Winshields Crags beckoning, as that talk with Sue buzzing in my head. It's the fix I needed to realise what's going on, that's getting me going. Everything out there is telling me something and I want to know what. On the way up, even three wild poppies make me pause and think.

XXXVIII SHORT CUTS

It should have been a short cut, up the hill opposite. But I've landed myself in a boggy area and pitch from tussock to tump, trying to keep my feet dry. It's an inconvenience, no more. When things are not straightforward though, my mind jumps on the bandwagon.

Water is oozing out of the rocks, so I recall a lucky escape when we didn't quite buy a house built over a water table. As I brush through undergrowth, I congratulate myself on wearing long trousers. That should keep the ticks at bay, as if an experience forty-odd year ago has any relevance today. As I climb, the rocky outcrops are in full sun. Somehow, I conjure up a picture of adders basking. Of course, there are none but, how is it I focus on the skull of what I take to be a dead rabbit? Come on now. The terrain is only a little tricky, but it's a war zone inside. I have to put a stop to this.

Flora comes to my rescue; plants. I'm treading on them. Some are quite pleasing to look at; four-petalled yellow jiggers here; a straggly purplish fellow there. And then I realise I don't have a clue. Names aren't my strong point. Ask me what one of these is called and I'll bumble – well, it looks like a small buttercup.

That's ridiculous. It's no such thing. Other names tumble out; sundew, vetch, asphodel – equally and stupidly wrong.

So what do I do? Wasn't there an Indian tribe that went on a long walk once a year with the very purpose of re-naming all that was familiar? There you are. I'll do my own thing. That four-petalled joker I'm calling ... suncup quadrefoil. The purple-flowered creeper I name ... velvet dewsip. I'm quite taken with this creative approach to plant identification. With ready-made names it's too easy to deal in stereotypes and take appearances for granted. I'm a four-leafed clover man. I've no wish to enter that coterie of labelled cosiness that stops you looking.

And then there are all the plants that are too easy to overlook, because they're not in flower, or don't. What about this spiky rush that you'd hardly entertain, were it not for its attentiveness? Soldier's lance, I'll call it. That seems appropriate. I look close. What I took to be discolouration of the stem turns out to be a light-winged insect; a lesser lancelot moth, if I'm not mistaken. When I look further, I realise there are many more nestling flush to each stem. One switch sends them flying. There must be hundreds here. What else, for want of looking, lies hidden; for want of questioning, remains unchallenged?

XXXIX SECOND OPINIONS

I've stopped for a rest by a pillar. It's a trig point and there's a great view. We may be a small island but there's infinity in all directions here. Then, these two women arrive. Before I know it, we're sitting down, chatting and my feet are still giving me gyp. I didn't expect a quick fix, of course, but I do happen to mention Sue's remedy.

'I don't think that's right at all,' the older woman says. 'You want blister plasters, that's what.'

'What? There are special plasters for blisters?'

'Yes, of course.'

'What about the ones I'm using? Aren't they any good?'

'Probably not. Zinc oxide, I expect. I don't think much of them. The blister ones are colloidal.'

'I see.' I don't, but keep my ignorance to myself. Strange thing is she puts me in mind of an older Sue, with hair gathered up at the back and, with specs, even more authoritative.

'Are you badly off? How many have you got?'

'Two.'

'Well, look. Here's three to tide you over.'

'So kind of you. Thanks so much.'

'But what you needed was blister preventative treatment.'

'Yes?'

'It's icy cold,' chimes in the younger companion, who turns out to be her daughter, 'and I screamed like hell when you applied it.'

'But people swear by it. They really do,' the mother assures.

If it hurts that much, I would think so.

Now, just as we're getting down to the nitty-gritty, the businesslike figure of another woman, with stick in hand, clomps towards us; a hill-climbing professional if ever I saw one. Keen as mustard, she muscles in on the blister talk.

'I use Vaseline,' she says.

In that one moment, I know three things:

1. She's Australian.
2. Australians don't hold back.
3. There's more than one way to catch a kangaroo.

'Vaseline's best. Been all over the place and I've had no trouble.'

'No?' I say, hard to believe it can be as simple as that.

'No,' she repeats. But, disappointingly, doesn't offer to grease my palm with a handy smear. 'Sticks are good too, specially for up-and-down hills like these. I've got just the one, but two are better; special cushioning ones, that save your knees.'

'Oh, not just ordinary then?'

'Heavens, no. Trekking poles.'

I hadn't given any thought to knees. Or saving them. Realisations are crowding in on me:

63   [DAY THREE]

1. Australians don't get bushwhacked.
2. Sticks can be fancy-dressed.
3. There's more to walking than two feet ... much, much more.

At this point, they're all nodding knowingly at me. At this point, I'm feeling unstuck, outsmarted and, frankly, a schmuck. There's only one way ... 'Well, must be pushing on, I suppose.'

I plod on, leaving the blister task force to continue its deliberations without me, my feet or, come to that, my knees.

XL FOOT SOLDIERS

We have to live with ups and downs. I'm aware of that. With their undulating spine, these hills have a fair few of them. So do my feet and it's becoming noticeably harder to negotiate the distance between a raised foot and the ground.

The negotiation goes something like this:

Me: 'There's a nice patch of grass in front of you. How about it?'

Feet: 'What's new?'

Me: 'Moving forward, that's new.'

Feet: 'Who's kidding? Heard it all before. Anyway, it looks like a bed of nails.'

Me: 'You're joking. Just try it, will you.'

Feet: 'What's it worth?'

And that's where the cost-benefit analysis breaks down. I can't buy them off. The feet are winning.

I try diversionary tactics. I meet a group of seven, chatting away animatedly by the Wall. 'Looks like a committee meeting,' I interject. 'Any chance of a decision?'

'Oh yeah,' the chairman says. 'We're going that-a-way.' He points in the direction of the pub. We laugh. But there's no getting away from my feet. The message is as crystal clear as if a small plane had flown past with a streamer advertising the Ten Commandments (abridged version). It reads, 'Thou shalt not.'

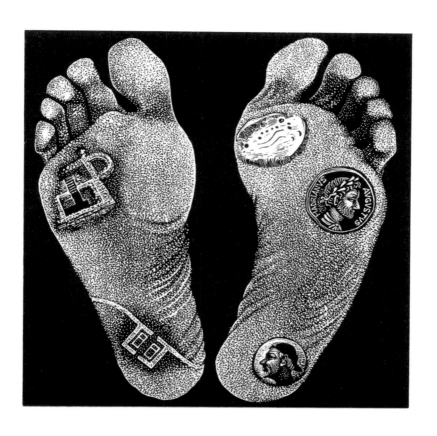

*'I ... try to persuade my feet that they belong in
the Roman Army Museum ...'*

It's 11.40 a.m. now. I had hoped to get to the Roman Army Museum – about six miles away, I guess – soon after lunch. When my feet were agreeable, three miles per hour was not unreasonable. With our differences of opinion, let's settle on one and a half miles per hour or half a mile (that's 880 yards, I reckon) every twenty minutes. Rounding down, that works out at around 40 paces a minute, or one pace every one and a half seconds. Looking down, and even allowing for my arithmetic, that sounds fast.

Hard as I might try to persuade my feet that they belong in the Roman Army Museum, getting them there before closing time looks like long odds. Until, that is, I remember a secret weapon; three of them in my pocket. I can do it now. Hitting upon a suitable rock for a seat, I set about stripping my feet, ready for the blister plasters. I'm gingerly pulling off that redundant zinc oxide stuff, when two women approach.

XLI PRIVATE TREATMENT

'Hallo again.'
'How is it? Putting the plasters on, are you?'
'Thought I might as well.'
She seems concerned. 'Got to be clean, you know.'
'I have those fresh-up things you use for your hands. Won't they do?'
She gives me one of those horrified expressions you'd give a llama that you don't know spits, until it does. 'You shouldn't be let out,' she says. 'Here, let's have a look. I've got some anti-bacterial wipes.' And, with that, she sits alongside and prepares for action.
'You're too kind,' I say. 'It'll hold you up.'
'Not half as much as it will you, if I don't. I'm a nurse.' You can't argue with a nurse. 'There are five,' she announces.
'Five?' I query, as if it's a new number.
'Three blisters here, two there. See?' I can't, but no wonder

there was discontent in the ranks. 'We should have enough blister plasters between us to do the job.'

I make a good out-patient from now on; keeping my mouth shut, observing procedures – the cleaning, wiping, dressing; comforted in the knowledge that no feet could get better treatment this side, or any side of Hadrian's Wall. All the while Pat is tending me (I know their names now), daughter Angie watches in a way that makes me think that this is their everyday routine.

Soon the last plaster's in place. Though I give them, of course, Pat doesn't want thanks; just best practice. 'Keep them dry,' she instructs, 'and your socks ... .'

Here goes. I've been playing with combinations: Bart out, thick in; Bart inside, thick out; and Bart by himself – to see if it made any difference. But I think she's spotted the Bart's.

' ... not up to much, are they? You need walking socks.'

'I see. What? Special ones ... for walking?'

'Yes. The double-looped type I'm wearing is fine.' She shows me. 'Two pairs. Not cheap but worth it. They help your feet breathe and take the pressure.' Then she tells me how to lace up the boots. 'You need the grip over the foot. That's where it has to be tighter, not so much over the front of the ankle. Feet are important. I've worked on them a lot. I practise reflexology, you see.'

XLII LETTING GO

I watch their heads drop below the ridge before I loosen up and let out one whoop. You people, you're great. You angels, you Nightingales. There I was, paddling in the pits and now I'm flying with the gods – well, almost. It's magic what one good turn will do. It's breaking out all over and ... oh dear ... is that a song coming on? Um ... *'Somewhere over the rainbow, stars shine bright ... um ... dum de, dum diddle um de, dum diddle ... what a sight. And then I wished upon a star ... the thing I wished, I wished you are ... beyond me.'* Sorry, Sue. It's Rainbow's end. This'll have to do.

But the euphoria remains. Walking is wonderful. It's the camaraderie, the people I meet, the club I've joined. Could I ever have imagined my feet receiving private treatment, right here on Hadrian's Wall? There's no question, last hill or not, this is a lemon drop moment. And the next mile or two, I'm in a haze of high hope. I could be walking over red hot coals and not know it. A refreshing breeze helps me on my way.

I come to a milecastle at Caw Gap. A display board reminds me that the Wall was built in short sections by regular army troops, with inscriptions often recording whose team carried out the work. So there you are. However arduous each pace of mine might be, it's as nothing compared with the time and effort those chaps spent building that pace in walling. It's not just stone. There are men's lives in there. And they deserve recognition. I leave a footprint. They've left a landmark.

Nearly two o'clock now and lunch is overdue. I'm approaching Cawfields Quarry car park, an ideal stop. There's a small lake, children paddling, a model boat or two and toilets. It's only when I spy a large rock that I realise eyes are trained on me. Who do I see sitting there? ... Pat and Angie. It's hard to avoid the suspicion that they've been awaiting my arrival.

'Hallo again. It's my turn to catch you up.'

'Yes. We're having a breather. How are you doing?'

'Managing OK, thanks to you. Bit of a hobble still, but nothing much.'

'We saw. You must expect that. It'll take a while.'

I sit beside them. We note how the quarry has cut into the run of the Wall. A shame, but it does show how intractable the terrain is and was, with scant earth overlying the bedrock. Digging footings can't have been easy.

Pat tells me a little more about herself. After nursing, she spent time teaching and remembers well a delinquent lot, bottom stream. 'But they were great,' she says. 'They saw me as a nurse, more than teacher. That helped.' I see how she acquired her patience ... and tenacity. Now she's working with the terminally ill and says she finds it rewarding. 'It's life's lessons you learn there.'

How fortunate to meet up with them again. What puts us on the same stretch of the Wall is as unfathomable as being here at all. Our time together might be short but there's a timelessness about it that I can't pin down, nor want to. I like the ease with which we meet and the thanks with which we say goodbye, letting come, letting go.

XLIII GAME POINTS

As I tuck into my packed lunch, these encounters get me thinking. Sue comes up with one solution and Pat with another. It's bizarre that I go along with the first and jump straight on board the second. Both might be valid, of course. But something about these experiences intrigues me. I feel like a player in some game where they've thrown away the rules. I have to pick them up. Think that's OK? Give it a try. That not working? Have a go at this. It's called life, isn't it?

There's another twist to this game. It's not clear what it is to win. This isn't *ludus latrunculorum*, the Soldier's Game. There's no enemy to capture. There was a destination, but the way the walk's developing, even that has faded. I've hardly thought about it. It's what the walk is turning into that's grabbing me now. The purpose is in the playing. The challenge is how.

In any game, it's how you respond to a situation that counts. When a well-equipped woman approaches on the path, two sharp-shooting breasts pointing straight at me are hard to ignore. I can't remember seeing any quite as aggressive as these. While we exchange pleasantries, I man the trenches.

'You have to keep your eyes open,' she says.

'I try,' I parry.

'I found two pieces of Samian ware yesterday.'

'No. Really?'

'Yes. By the side of the path, that tell-tale terracotta colour, shiny, just a little embedded. Then another piece.'

'You'd hardly believe it possible, would you? I mean, after all this time and on the surface.'

'Why do you think so many molehills have been kicked?'

'Do you know, I hadn't even noticed.' I'm trying hard not to.

'People are always looking. You never know what you might see.'

'No. That's true. Well, good luck.'

And, off she goes, with her two treasures, while I vow to keep my eyes … on the ground.

XLIV DIVERTING TACTICS

Crossing a stile, I meet a middle-aged chap walking by himself. 'From Cornwall, but not Cornish,' he tells me, and 'you must travel the Carlisle to Settle line over the Dales. It's so scenic, you mustn't miss it. Only one and a half hours each way.'

Here's a test. I could carry on regardless. But if I don't follow up suggestions like this, I'm not playing the game, not seeing what happens when something turns up. If I don't do it, I'll be none the wiser. If I do and nothing much comes of it, what have I lost? Three hours perhaps, a few quid and a misapprehension or two. I can live with that. It's a diversion I'll make time for. We don't walk together very far. His pace is too quick for me, so I wave him on; a retired stockbroker, I deduce, out of sorts in shorts. I imagine him striding off in pinstripes.

Soon I'm threading past a farmhouse and the scarcely visible signs of Great Chesters Fort. You wouldn't know, unless someone told you, that 480 auxiliaries were garrisoned here, though there's a fenced-off area in a field which, a couple tell me, screens an underground store.

Out in the open, I have other concerns: I'm under attack. A flock of black-headed sheep is pelting towards me from behind, baaing their heads off. It's a stampede. Quick, or I'll be mown down. A few nifty sidesteps and I just manage to avoid being woolsacked. The good farmer brings up the rear.

'What's got into them?'

'They be all mixed up,' he laughs. 'Trying to find their lambs, that's it.'

Man worried by sheep, that's me. Self-respect demands that I try and get in a bit of sheep-worrying myself. A little further on, I steal up on one that's facing away from me, in mid-baa. Yes, a personal best. I'm within six yards before it gets wind of me and bleats a retreat. I'm sharpening up on covert operations.

XLV THE LOOKOUT

Talk about covert. Before I start an ascent, I happen to glance up. What I see in a rocky recess makes me smile, then burst out laughing. By the time I get there, I'm in a frivolous mood.

'Not you two again, is it? We can't go on meeting like this. I think you're spying on me.'

'Hah. Just had our lunch break, that's all.'

'What? This late? It's nearly four o'clock.'

'We can wait, can't we Angie. Women can.'

Angie nods. 'You're talking to someone who did the Macchu Picchu trek last year.'

'You did, Angie? Must have been impressive.'

She tells me about it.

'I want to go.'

'It was tough. The air is thin. But worth it, every step.'

'I bet. I've been tested too. Had to run for my life back there.'

'Yes?'

'This flock of sheep. After my blood, they were. Out of control. I don't know how the farmer copes. Insurrection it was.'

'It's karma,' Pat explains, entering into the spirit.

That's all I need to spark me off. 'Perhaps I was a sheep-worrier. Perhaps he was a centurion who mistreated his men.' Perhaps … perhaps. Where does it stop? And then I have to tell them about the conjunction of a wheel with a dual carriageway. 'Was I let off. Good karma, I suppose. Hope I haven't spent it.'

Pat and Angie indulge my ramblings up to a point. 'The Australian girl passed by not long ago. We had a chat.'

'Yes? Shame I missed her.'

'Oh look.' Pat breaks off. 'D'you see that?' She points. 'A red kite. Beautiful. Not many years ago, we spotted an eagle here. You'd be lucky to see one now.'

'It's still a great place, isn't it. Peaceful and majestic. It needs eagles.'

We fall quiet. They pick themselves up, ready to go.

'It's been marvellous meeting you both. Thanks again. But I'll know where to find you next time – hidden in a crevice, waiting to pounce. I'll look out for you. G'bye then.'

'Bye.'

And no one as much as mentioned feet.

XLVI HARD LABOUR

A man is poring over the information board at Walltown Crags Turret. I've just read it and can't imagine what's detaining him. He walks away a short distance, then returns and reads again. What has he found? Something he doesn't understand or something so interesting it went clean over my head? A female companion further on hasn't been zapped by the board and looks round every so often, as impatient to continue their walk as I am curious about what's keeping him. I backtrack.

'Excuse me.' I interrupt his stoop, which disguised his true height; a deal taller than my six feet. In his 40s, I would say, athletic sort, with a ring of dark hair round an arid plateau. For want of a clue to his absorption, I can only trot out, 'Fascinating, isn't it.'

'How they can do thish?' he quizzes me. Probably German, I

think. Austrian possibly. Maybe Dutch.

'No. I don't know,' shaking my head, not knowing what 'thish' they've done.

'I had friend … have friend in Pyrenees, help … helped build shtone house for heem last year. We pick shtone from quarry – hash to be flat top and bottom, takes … took time finding good type. Then, one at a time on to lorry – awf again other end, on pile. Then shtart building, pick over shtones, shoose right one, not any – up ladder, no, not right – back down, pick other one – up ladder, put down, re-range, not still OK – down, up, down. Maybe 15 times,' he shrugs, 'each shtone picked over, pick up, put down, from shtart to end. Hard, I tell you. One daysh work, three daysh back pain.' He holds his back in anguish. 'And they do thish?' A sweeping gesture at the Wall. 'Amaschzing.'

His teeth seem to get in the way of the words. But that creates a gritty, clenched type of speech that goes well with the painful process he describes. And, really there isn't much more to say. I could have said about carts, not lorries. I might have mentioned that the Romans, with their organisation, probably got it down to less than 15, but why? He'd said it all, forcefully enough, and I didn't need to read what I'd missed, what I thought I already knew. How many read about the Wall and just see measurements? Those words weren't dead to him. He'd done it. He knew what they meant. And now he'd given vent, he was free to travel on.

It helps me too on my final limp to the Roman Army Museum. I am reminded what work is. It's 5.30 p.m. when I arrive but I've got them here, the feet, an hour before closing time.

'Is it too late to look round properly?' I ask at the desk.

'Really, yes,' they say. 'You need one and a half hours, possibly two.' They don't seem happy.

XLVII HOTTING UP

'OK, I'll come back tomorrow. What time d'you open?'
    'Ten o'clock.'

I see a refreshment area. 'D'you do breakfasts by any chance?'

'We can rustle up a toastie, if that'll do.'

'That's good of you.'

They are helpful, but still serious.

'Have you done much more business then, since the path opened?'

'None.'

'No? Why ever not?'

'They've put us down as a car park and toilet, not a museum, that's why.'

'What? That's crazy.'

'Yes. We're not best pleased.'

'I should think not.' I can see why they're steamed up.

'I've booked into a barn tonight,' I tell them, 'at Greenhead. There's a sleeping bench, whatever that is. If it's anything like I imagine, odds on I'll be between two snorers. My wife says I snore. She does but I don't. I haven't heard myself once.'

'You wouldn't, would you?' At last, some smiles.

'Is it far to Greenhead?'

'No. Left out of the entrance, then over the stile and down the hill.'

'Thanks. See you tomorrow.'

The barn has three mattresses on a long wooden plinth and a bunk bed. And, glory be, I'm the only occupant, so it's the top bunk for me, chaps, and no snoring. Actually, I wouldn't have minded some company, but there's time to relax now, before I make the very welcome friend of a dinner at the village pub.

Time, too, to collect my thoughts. Despite the best efforts of Sue and Pat, it's taken seven hours to walk from Twice Brewed to the Museum, with stops, granted. That's about one mile per hour, a crawl. I'm coming to the conclusion that the boots are making things worse. My feet are overheating. It's like the prickly heat when you walk on white sand in high summer.

My boots don't breathe, that's the trouble, and my feet are

suffocating. I've got to get some lighter footwear. But where? Out here, the closest I can get to a shoe shop is a strip of local cow hide, and the cow wouldn't like it. What would I give to slip on those sandals skulking at the bottom of the wardrobe back home? Like most people must have – probably half forgotten. Which gives me an idea …

XLVIII OPPORTUNIST KNOCK

I can feel the resolve growing as I shuffle towards the pub. It's bold and a bit of a cheek perhaps, but this is the game plan. I'll knock on doors in the village and ask each occupier whether he or she might possibly be about to throw out an old pair of sandals. The one thing people don't do is chuck out the old when they buy new. The easy-going familiarity between well-worn footwear and feet is not readily forgone. Mine continue doing good service in the garden long after they should have been slung. So there's a hope that I'll strike lucky.

A row of Victorian terraced houses fronts the road. Which door shall I knock? The very first in the row? No. That's far too methodical – like working your way through the peas before starting on the carrots. I'll feel my way into the first knock. And there, staring me in the face, about half way along, is a gift. An old upright vacuum cleaner has been left outside a front door, a candidate for a car boot sale if ever there was. What else might follow? But not just that. The front door is ajar – about a quarter open – enough for someone to quickly knock and put a head round, as one does when almost half-invited. Which is exactly what I do.

'Is anyone there?'

A cough from within. 'There is,' a voice comes, followed by a lady in her mid-years, looking cheerfully preoccupied. 'Yes?'

'Uh … I see you're getting rid of a vacuum cleaner.'

'What?' She laughs. 'That's the chimney sweep's.' And, with that, she opens the door a little wider. Over her shoulder – she's not tall – straight in front of me is a flight of stairs, and at the bottom of the stairs, tucked in close at the foot of the bottom step, are not one, but two pairs of sandals – men's.

IL CLEAN SWEEP

'It wasn't the vacuum cleaner actually. It's my feet playing up. You see, I've been walking the Path and these boots are chronic. I can't go on like it and wondered if you'd possibly have an old pair of sandals you might be getting rid of.'

'There's my husband's sandals. Here.' She points.

'Well, I never,' shaking my head. 'Two pairs.'

'Yes, but he's not in.'

'Oh. You wouldn't know whether he wears them both, I suppose?'

'I don't, I'm afraid.' She looks perplexed and there are scuffling sounds inside. 'Look, you'd better come in. This is Bert.'

Bert is busy pushing canes through a ragged hole in what looks like a 50s curtain remnant.

I can't think of anything better to say than, 'Hallo Bert. Going OK, is it?'

'Thanks.' Bert looks everything a chimney sweep should.

She's full of praise. 'Previous chap was no good. You should see how much soot Bert's getting.' There's a healthy kerplumph of soot down the chimney.

'My word, yes. And so clean too.'

'But about the sandals ... ,' she kindly remembers, ' ... it's a bit difficult, him not being here. Perhaps you could hire them for the night, could you?'

'Well, possibly. Actually, I was hoping ...'

'And then you could pop them back tomorrow.'

'I suppose I could. But d'you think he would miss them, just one pair, the more worn ones like ... if they are, I mean? But what would you say to him? I can quite see it's not easy when he comes back, explaining you've let a strange bloke who knocked on your door borrow his sandals for the night.'

She gets up, goes to the stairs, picks up one pair and, on impulse, 'Why don't you try them on anyway?'

Black, I observe. 'Would you believe it? They match my trousers.'

'So they do.'

And the size? I shove a foot in one. 'Look at that. Perfect.'

L FIRST ROUND

She addresses the chimney. 'What do you think, Bert?'

'See you through the winter all right it will, Mrs.'

Bert has, all the time, been oblivious to the mini-drama being played out around him, staying focussed as a professional sweep would on screwing and unscrewing canes, not scrambling sandals.

'Yes,' she says, and turning to me, 'well, tell you what; Geoff's working at the Greenhead pub down the road. Why don't you go and ask him yourself?'

'That's funny. I was going there anyway. But how will I know who he is?'

'You can't miss him. He's got ginger hair and he's bald.'

'OK.'

It doesn't seem right to stomp off just like that, so we chat a little, while Bert finishes his canework. They moved from Whitley Bay, I gather, and she's into birdwatching. I talk about red kites and eagles. She says she's seen a merlin and, in one last attempt to draw Bert into the conversation, she asks, 'Have you seen a merlin, Bert?'

'Black, is it?'

She leaves him to get on with the clearing up and, with vacuum cleaning imminent, that's my cue to be off.

'Shall I take the sandals with me then?'

'Might as well, since you're wearing them. Tell him Eileen sent you.'

'OK. Thanks so much. Bye Bert.'

It's a short walk to the pub and, in the sandals, cool. They're busy. People are well into their first course. Christmas turkey-size plates remind me of another mission. There are two barmen. One is a black-haired young chap. The other is older. That has to be him – a cheerful Des O'Connor sort of face, with close-cut scalp, sprouting what could pass as a first flush of fair to auburn hair, hardly ginger. It could be the light.

'You Geoff?'

'That's right.'

'I've got three requests.' I can't come straight to the point, can I?

'First, a lemonade and lime, if you don't mind. Half will do.'

'Certainly. No trouble.'

'And then, can I order a lasagne, like that one over there, with the garlic bread?'

'Of course you can. Take about 25 minutes it will, if that's all right.' It's not getting easier.

'Yes?'

'Oh, and the last. It's this. I've been walking … the Path.' I lift up the boots I've been dangling below the counter. 'They've been giving me real gyp, and well … Eileen asked me to ask you if you still needed these?' I hoick up one leg, so he can see. 'Your sandals.'

LI SMALL WORLD

Geoff is taken aback. If the hairs on his head could rise up, they would. Thoughtless of me. It wasn't a good idea doing this to him in a public bar, but I can't stop now.

'I happened to spot them at the bottom of the stairs while the chimney was swept. Eileen let me try them on. Good of her, wasn't it.' I can see he's under pressure. There are other customers waiting.

'Just a minute,' he splutters. 'If you like to sit down, I'll bring your drink. That's 65p then.'

'Thanks, Geoff.'

'Will there do?' He motions to a nearby table where one girl is sitting.

'After that, any table will do.' What must he be thinking? I sit down, look up and there's a ruddy face in front of me. Familiar.

'Goodness.' It's the Australian girl. 'We met on Whin Sill, didn't we?'

'Yuh, so we did.'

'Fancy meeting you here.' I talk about a small world.

Geoff is arriving with the drink, over my shoulder. He plonks it down. 'There. Do you do this often?' he says.

'I try not to.'

'Well, tell you what. You can have 'em.'

'What?' I say. 'That's fantastic. I must give you something.'

'Don't mention it. It's on me. Next drink could be pricey though.'

'It'll be worth every penny, Geoff. Really. Thanks.'

I'm taken aback now. When what you hope for happens, it has a whiff of the miraculous. Or, in my case, when you manage to hold on to what you've got.

LII ROUND TABLE

The talk is flowing now. The beer too. Travelling looms large. Cathy, it is, has been through Asia, plans a trip to Southern Ireland after this, before she tackles the rest of Europe. She always camps wherever she goes, sometimes a site, sometimes a farmer's field, never books up.

'For a woman,' I say, 'alone, isn't that risky?'

'Australian, remember,' she replies. No answer to that.

'So what do you carry then?'

'18 kilos.'

'That's some weight.'

My paltry eleven kilos are heavy enough, but no complaints about shoulder problems from the Vaseline queen. She loves the life, would live it forever if she could.

I'm caught up with her enthusiasm. 'I'd like to see Australia, but I can't stand the heat.'

'Come to Melbourne in winter then. It might be cold, wet and miserable, but there are some nice parts.'

That's a bit of a slap-down for a softie. They make 'em tough down under. No nos for an answer.

Time for another drink. Their best bitter gets better. But, am I seeing things already? I'm certainly hearing an unmistakable voice. Right alongside, at the bar, appears a chap who knows a thing or two about moving stones and with him, his partner.

'Hi! Well, how about that? You'll never guess what's happening. There's a reunion going on. Here, meet Cathy.'

I don't catch it clearly, but he's something like Abraham and his wife is Immy. We're into serious bonhomie.

LIII OFF BALANCE

The beer is just about keeping up with the conversation. They're going to Ireland too, tomorrow. Cathy's pleased to hear that. There's a mention of Amsterdam – yes, they are Dutch – and of the walk many people do; the pilgrim's route to Santiago de Compostela.

'Shirley MacLaine's done it,' Immy says. 'She's written a book.'

Immy's a musician. She looks like she belongs on a Swiss alpine slope, a Heidi, with blonde hair and plait. We never learn what Abraham does. It must be either quality control work – I can see him doing time and motion studies – or perhaps team building ... with stones.

We tackle the work/life balance. Cathy says it should be all life. I say balance.

Immy impresses me. 'Not everyone needs to balance. Work

might be everything.' She's good like that, stopping you in your tracks, coming up with something in counterpoint, like a musician would.

I say, 'Whenever you're doing anything, there's always something else you want to do,' and tell them my joke about the committee meeting on the Wall and how they vote for the pub, when the dinner party takes a surreal turn. I'm half expecting a reprise of that scene in *Beetlejuice* when they all get up and dance round the table hysterically, singing that calypso, '*Day-o, day-ay-ay-o. Daylight come and me wanna go home.*' Except I don't. I look over to the bar and do a double take. Standing there are two of the committee.

LIV WELCOME RELIEF

It's not the beer, good though it is. It's them. But then, in the way one quickly acclimatises to spirits, it's a casual, 'Ah, hallo again. You made it.'

Meanwhile, back at the conversation, the food's arrived, plates piled high and wide. I say, 'I did warn you. There's enough for one between two.'

'We'll manage,' says Abraham.

'I'm sure you will.'

Abraham, if I hadn't already guessed, is a deep thinker. Out of the blue, he fixes his eyes on me. 'What are your motives?'

That unnerves me. What is this? A googly? I don't know how to bat, so I take him to mean motivation. 'I like putting things together in a different way,' I say obliquely.

'Sho chaotic?' he summarises.

'Well, yes, I suppose. But … no. It all starts with chaos. I like finding order.'

'Or more chaos?' says Immy.

'Perhaps … a different kind of chaos.'

The beer is good.

I'm at the bar again, when a chap comes up to me and says to his wife, 'Look who's here.' I am baffled. I cannot remember these people. I don't recognise them. Besides, this reunion thing is getting beyond a joke. Past lifetimes are ganging up on me.

'You know, we met you twice, on the Wall and at Twice Brewed.'

'Yes?' I query.

'Yes.' The man is so insistent. Perhaps I do know him. Perhaps he knows me. After all, there are two of them and only one of me.

I do him a favour. I help him out. 'Ah yes. Let me see. What was it we talked about now? Blisters, wasn't it?' I know a safe bet when I see one.

'Yes, yes. Blisters,' he says.

'Blisters,' I repeat, melting into the distance.

'Are you OK?'

'Working on it, I'd say.' Am I relieved. Blisters save the day. He seems happier, now he thinks that I know I know them. But it's me who's worried. I still can't place these people. My mind's wandered. 'See you again sometime. You never know.'

LV CHEERS EVERYONE!

And then, at the table – well, it had to happen – my fault, I expect: blisters pop up again. Abraham is saying how he walked 30 kilometres on a blister with only Vaseline. Cathy is nodding vigorously and Immy comes up with this 'second skin' business. 'That's what you need.'

'Second skin?' I screw up my face. 'Haven't heard of it.'

'Look. I have one on my elbow.' She shows me.

'Aah, I see.' She means a blister plaster.

'We must give you some,' she insists.

'No. Please,' I say. I don't like to let on that I'm already wearing them and there's only so much kindness I can take. Luckily, Cathy keeps quiet. 'No. I couldn't possibly. You might

need them in Ireland. I can manage, really, now I have sandals.'
I lift up my foot. 'See. Thanks to Geoff.' I glance towards the bar.
It's getting beyond me. He's talking … to Eileen.

Seeing me, she comes over. 'You're OK then?'

'Absolutely fine, thanks. Geoff said I can have them. It's so
kind of him.' I drop my voice. 'I'd like to give him something
for his trouble, but he won't take anything. Look, if I give you a
tenner, d'you think you could slip him something … secretly?'

'You can buy me a drink, if you like.'

That's what I like; down-to-earthiness, all the way from Whitley
Bay. 'Yes. Sure. Geoff too, of course. Here, have whatever you
like, whatever's yours. Oh, I'll have another too.' It's, 'Thanks
again, Geoff,' when the drink arrives.

'You'll look after them, won't you?' he says. 'They came all
the way from Devon.'

'Hah. That's where they'll be going. Home.'

Cathy has to go now and then the others. We shake hands. It's
'Good Luck' and 'Safe Journey' all round.

'Cheers, everyone.' I could kiss the lot of them.

LVI WAKE-UP CALLS

Over at the barn, I'm trying to organise a good night's sleep,
before the local mice get their barn dance going. It's the
gap below the door that'll let them in. I should be spared their
attentions on the top bunk but, all the same, I plug the gap with
some bags of tile grout and adhesive that are lying around.

Soon I'm ready to settle down for the night, thoughts full of
how I came by my most prized possession, black sandals, and
the great people I've met today who seem to have been lifelong
friends. But I've hardly dropped off when there's a loud squawk
from outside, a bird perturbed by the sound of it. It must have
some axe to grind because, give or take a few minutes, it squawks
again and, give a few more, again and again.

Now this wouldn't be so bad, were it not for some serious

nagging at the foot of the bed, or more precisely at the foot of my left foot. It's a throb that won't listen to reason, any more than the bird responds to my mental dead-heading. What perverse bird squawks all night? I'd like to know.

I must be meant to pay attention. Mine is not a gasp of enlightenment, more a dull, sickening groan. My mind goes back to the puncturing and the blister I didn't cut open … on the left foot. I'm thinking scissors. I'm thinking unsterilised. I'm thinking I didn't think. Pat might have cleaned the outside of that blister but little bleeders had already got in, that's what. Where wipes couldn't swipe – inside – there are now little breeders, flourishing in the tropical climate furnished by my boots. They'd have nasty-sounding names that probably end in 'coccus' and rhyme with 'sock us' and 'fock us'. It's the gatecrashers you never would see that you want to worry about.

The night is lying like Old Brer Rabbit with all four feet in the air, pretending to be dead. It fooled Brer Fox. Me too. When a cat starts scratching at the barn door and then a large black beetle scurries across the floor, like a hearse in a hurry, the message is loud and clear: I'd better get up.

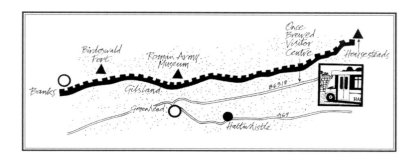

DAY FOUR

'A new situation need only be a touch different from the old for one not to make the connection.'

LVII RECYCLING HISTORY

I have breakfast. Dunking a cookie in a cup of tea does it and I do what all hikers do in times of crisis – I pack and re-pack my rucksack. The boots are at the bottom. Tile grout and adhesive bags back where I found them and I'm ready. I open the door in time for a fly-past by two house martins on a home buyers' recce, before they exit and I perform the closing ceremony. There's finality about closing a door. I need to move on. I need a doctor. I need feet.

There's no doctor locally, the barn lady advises. She suggests I try Haltwhistle Health Centre, about three miles away. I can catch a 685 bus at 9.30. That gives me some time. I look round the remains of the 14th century Thirlwall Castle nearby. There are so many places with 'wall' to their names; so many buildings with Hadrian's Wall to their walls and this castle more than most. If only Hadrian had known what else his stone would build. How much is history recycled.

Before I catch the bus, I call my next B & B at Banks to book an evening meal. We agree on a 'no frills' chicken salad. 'I may be a bit late,' I say. 'Around fiveish, I think.' But I haven't worked out yet how I'm going to get there.

Then, while I'm waiting at the bus stop, striding towards me come Abraham and Immy. I am not surprised. This bumping into people I know is getting commonplace. It's great to see them again though. They slept overnight in their car and are looking for breakfast. The pub's closed and they can't hold on for a ten o'clock toastie at the Army Museum, as I suggest.

'No. I'll have to drop in later,' I tell them, not letting on about the feet. I think I've played out that topic. They're off to the nearest town to get a bite, then Ireland. Good to feel the warmth of last night still close.

But it's made me think. Now I've boarded the bus, I'm bemused. I'm wrestling questions that keep coming back. What am I up to? What is this journey I'm on? And what happened last night that can tell me?

I needed sandals and felt positive about finding them. But how the need was met still dumbfounds me. I could not have expected the answer to be so direct, more immediate even than Sue saying to friends, 'Meet me in Carlisle with a trailer and £500.' I had no friends to ask to turn up with sandals but there they were, waiting for me. Sandals and friends.

LVIII UNTHINKING THOUGHTS

Do I accept these events and travel on regardless? I can't. I'm not made that way. Take the barn. I anticipated trouble: snorers first, then mice. The blighters (mice, that is) used to invade an old timber cottage I rented in my student days. Nothing stopped them. They were always rustling about in the wastepaper basket or scavenging for kitchen scraps. I used to pull the sheet over my head to shut out the scrabbling, though it didn't stop the thought of them scampering over the bed. Thirty odd years ago, I'd been conditioned to expect trouble. That's exactly what I got in the barn and the feedback in squawks and throbs fulfilled my worries about a sleepless night wonderfully.

I had no such apprehensions with the sandals. I expected success. I had sandals sculling about at home. So would others. But what if I'd had doubts? I could have conjured up a catalogue. I might have thought of all the doors I'd have to knock before I found someone with, not just sandals, but a spare pair. Even then, would they be prepared to part with them and for how much? And what if they were the wrong size? And what about asking? If I'd known I'd have to ask a barman in a public bar whether I could keep his sandals that I was already wearing, would I have knocked at all?

But there's more to my manufacturing. People might have thought I was out of order asking, or pulling a fast one. They might have slammed the door in my face and reported this bogus caller, with a new line in scams, to the police. If I'd run my head through this lot, who knows where I'd have ended up?

Not with a decent pair of sandals, that's for sure.

So, was the way it turned out down to a lucky break? I don't think so. Wasn't it because I didn't play consequences? Desperate for relief, I saw sandals as my salvation and took the first step that held out any hope. That's all. I only had to knock – once as it happened – to make everything else possible. That's the point. It's taken me halfway through the walk to realise it. It's the first step that counts, the one that stares you in the face. Take it, again and again, and nothing can hold you back. That's how to play the game I'm on. It ought to be RULE ONE.

LIX CENTRAL POINT

Thinking all this, there's not one thing I notice on the bus trip to Haltwhistle until I arrive and then haven't a clue which is the right stop for the Health Centre. The driver doesn't know but a lady behind speaks up. 'I'll tell you where to get off.' I like the way she says it.

Haltwhistle is a market town at the centre of Britain, it is claimed. It doesn't escape me that the Health Centre must be Britain's *most* central. Seeing the receptionist tapping data into a computer though, I resist the temptation to tease with, 'I suppose you suffer a bit from over-centralisation.'

Soon I am registered as an unhealthy visitor and wait my turn, in a hush helped by a video loop about breast screening. A sign which flashes up 'Next patient for open surgery' worries me more. There's distraction in the prints on the walls. A Mark Rothko, *No.10 – 1950* catches my eye. There's an indefinable something about the colours. Then a Nicholas Verrall, *Un pichet de limonade* (I must be thirsty) and finally, on my short list, a print of some blue shuttered doors that I fancy, instead of the nondescript one I am called to come through.

The diagnosis is remarkably in line with my own, but the doctor's plain speaking rings like a revelation. 'Basically, you've got ruddy big holes in your feet which, not surprisingly, let in a whole lot of germs and infection.' I keep quiet about the scissors. Checking that I'm not allergic to penicillin, he puts me on a course of antibiotics and Ibuprofen, to do a better job than Paracetamol of stopping the throb.

I'm directed to the hospital, not far away, for the blisters to be treated and re-dressed. 'They'll see if they can come up with a dressing for the awkward spot below the toes,' he says.

It's less than half an hour since I first arrived and already the nurse is doing her best to negotiate the rugged terrain underfoot. NHS, I'm impressed. 'Keep the plasters on for a few days at least,' she advises. 'Your feet need to be out of water, so baths are better than showers, and walk as little as possible.'

'What? That was the whole point,' I feel like saying, but don't. Nor do I ask about the plasters. With apologies to Pat, the question of whether they are zinc oxide or colloidal doesn't seem that crucial.

LX COMMUNITY SPIRIT

The hospital dispensary sorts out the antibiotics, but I can buy the Ibuprofen in town. 'Cheaper,' they say. That means finding a chemist on foot. The thought of the walk is enough for me to ditch the idea. I'll cope with the throb.

Instead, I'm going to treat my feet. They've had a lot to put up with. 'Know where I can get some socks?' I ask a passer-by.

'The shop over there might have them. It's closing down though. Don't know if much is left.'

This time, the socks have to be right. I browse the half-empty racks. There is one pair of walking socks left; not double loop, it's true, but at half price, my size and black, they'll do nicely. My feet and I are relieved.

Antibiotics next, but they're to be taken after a meal. At the least, I need to drink. One shop along – run in aid of some charity – people are sipping tea. This will do. I pop in, but all the tables are occupied. One seat remains where three women are sitting.

'All right here?' I ask.

'Oh yes,' I'm invited. One look and one listen suggest I have redoubtable company. It's not a question of breaking into the conversation, more being enveloped.

Straight away, I'm pitched into the 'Haltwhistle's-such-a-lovely-place-to-live' audio-visual promotion. 'Everyone's so helpful and friendly. Wonderful community spirit here,' one formidable lady says. It's with me already. My cup of tea and biscuits arrive almost before I order them and I'm being asked how my walk is going.

'There's a lot I could say but you haven't got all day, have you, ladies?' I tantalise.

'Oh no. We've a busy day ahead.'

I give them a taster.

'But have you been to Vindolanda?' the lady on my left petitions, and without waiting, 'It's a wonderful place.'

'I know. I went. More people should see what they've found. It's incredible.'

'Isn't it,' she replies. 'I worked there fifteen years. And, you know, on the first day Robin Birley put some leather into my palm and said, "That would have been around at the time of Christ." Makes you think, that does.'

Fortuitous to meet someone who spent much of her working life there and we're straight into some heavy eulogising. She's a fount of knowledge. With Abraham's probing fresh in mind, I ask about the wall stone. 'How did they quarry it?'

'They hammered wooden pegs into the joints of the rock, then let the frosts get to work, to split them open.'

'Simple, isn't it, when you know how.'

All good things come to an end. 'I've got to ring for the taxi,' says the lady on the right, reaching for her mobile. 'My husband,' she tips me off.

'That's what you call him?'

'Not always, and not to his face mind.'

I tell them I'm off to the Army Museum. Vindolanda lady says she knows them well. 'You'll meet a girl called Margie, I expect.'

'I might have met her already.'

'Say hello from me. They're all so cheerful.'

Mr. Taxi's not long – must be well trained – and three stalwarts of the Haltwhistle community are off, leaving me to plan the rest of the day … oh, and take my antibiotics.

LXI FOLLOWING THROUGH

It's no distance to the bus stop for the 11.25 Hopper to the Army Museum sited at Carvoran, near Greenhead. I'll need a couple of hours to do it justice, but the chances of walking from there to my next B & B look remote. I'll never make it in time and it won't do my feet any favours. It rankles but I'll have to hop on a bus again. Bussing offers one blessing though. When I walk, there's too much to notice. On a bus, the view changes too fast to pay attention. I can string thoughts together.

As town turns to country, my mind travels back to this morning. It might well have been orchestrated: from the first step, consulting the doctor, to the hospital, the one pair of walking socks and the one seat next to the Vindolanda lady. How did things work out so right? And why question it? Great British restraint has a lot to answer for. Too much of a good thing and we're ill at ease. Offer us another fresh cream cake and it's 'I oughtn't really but oh, if you insist, well all right, just this once.'

It's the double helping of right socks and seat that's rocked me – being in the right place at the right time twice. And that after the sandal business. I don't know how it's happened, any more than a homing pigeon knows how to find the loft. It's doing what comes naturally. Perhaps what I'm hitting on *should* come naturally.

But how does it happen? If this is a crash course in synchronicity, I hope they cover the theory. If I look for a clue, where there's an obvious choice, I've simply gone along with events. Following through with a 'go-ahead' gut feeling, one opportunity has led to the next.

I remember an old boss of mine explaining 'follow through'. With him, everything was golf. 'You've hit the ball. Does it matter what happens after?' he'd challenge. 'Of course it does. The stroke doesn't stop with the hitting. Letting your back foot off the ground helps keep balance and completing the swing is all part of the action that takes the ball to the green.' Get off your backsides, follow up your leads and clinch sales; that was his lesson.

Well, I'm not clinching sales, or teeing off. Not walking Hadrian's Wall Path, for that matter. Not any more. There is still a finishing post – Bowness – but the way things happen is what interests me now. If there's a RULE TWO to this game, it's a funny one. What shall I say? Act on your feelings and don't think too much if you want to find yourself where you feel you belong.

LXII SOLDIER'S LOT

The Museum comes as some relief to this heady stuff. Margie remembers the Vindolanda lady well and me only too well, especially the snoring.

'No. No one else at the barn, thank goodness. No snores. Not even me,' I assure her.

'Hah, hah.' I don't think she believes me.

'I had to keep the mice out though. Lucky I was on top bunk, with shiny metal posts they couldn't have climbed.'

'Want to bet?' she rejoins.

My visit starts with a superb eighteen-minute film showing an eagle's eye view of Hadrian's Wall. The legions adopted the eagle, which was associated with the most powerful Roman god, Jupiter Optimus Maximus (Best and Greatest), presiding as he did over storms, thunder and lightning. The eagle was assigned to collect Jupiter's thunderbolts. No other bird was surely worthy enough for such a mission. I am so impressed with the film that I decide on a second viewing later, if only to see one sweep from the air make light of my laboured footsteps.

In the meantime, I get absorbed in body armour with

splendidly evocative names such as *Lorica Squamata* (metal scales sewn on a linen undergarment), *Lorica Hamata* (a type of chain mail and stronger), *Lorica Cuirass* (solid metal front, fit for an emperor) and *Lorica Segmentata* (steel strips mounted on a leather harness). Tricky trade-offs there must have been between heavyweight protection and lightweight flexibility.

There's plenty more to see: a chariot, cavalryman with horse, displays of weaponry and a large scale model of a fort. But it is a copy of the soldiers' joining-up oath – 'I vow to serve the Emperor and the people of Rome' it starts – that makes me curious to mug up on the soldiers' life. How did they serve? They had to sign up for 25 years' service apparently, on completion of which they received Roman citizenship plus a grant of land to farm or cash in lieu. Only on completion too was marriage allowed or a previous 'unofficial' marriage and children legitimised.

But what of day-to-day realities? Not much respite from work, it seems. The working day was from dawn to dusk, with sick parade one hour before dawn. Combat and fitness training figured largely in their regular routine as did parades and practising manoeuvres. There were frequent route marches of up to 25 miles in full kit. They even had to swim in full kit. Nor were they just soldiers. Many were skilled tradesmen, in stonemasonry, plastering and shoemaking, for example.

A contribution towards the cost of armour and weapons was taken from soldiers' pay, as was a subscription to a 'burial club' to finance a respectable funeral, at which professional mourners might be hired to weep and wail. Perhaps soldiers ought to have been cheered on their way. For many, that might have been the closest to a peaceful retirement. Puts one's own paltry predicaments in perspective, doesn't it?

LXIII ABOUT TURN

I refill at the coffee shop before bidding goodbye, in time to catch the 15.13 bus to my next stop. The trusty Hopper arrives on the dot. 'Brocolitia?' I say. It's another fort I want to see.

'No. That's the next bus – 30 or 40 minutes.'

I step back confused. I'd read the timetable, but OK, I made a mistake. So be it. Then, after he drives off, and only then, a smoulder suddenly combusts. Aaah ... what? It was the right bus. I meant to say Birdoswald. Two bloody B's: that's all it takes to put me off my stroke. Bugger.

My time is short. Shall I wait? No. I'm blowed if I will. The next one could be a while. I'll try hitch-hiking. As people leave the Museum, I sidle up and ask. Every man jack of them would if they could but sorry, they can't. Any other direction fine. But mine? No.

I get involved in a lengthy conversation with one gent who's excited about having discovered Rome (as if he stumbled across it by accident), only to see another bus arriving. I cut him short. 'Excuse me. Might be mine.'

I hustle over. It's a 185. This time I'm emphatic, 'Uh, driver. Birdoswald Fort?'

'Near enough, ya.'

'Great.'

That little hiccup sorted, I jump on board and breathe the same sigh of satisfaction you get from finding lost specs perched on your nose ... except that, some way on, it appears that he's taking a round-the-houses route. It's leading to somewhere that looks suspiciously like somewhere I've been before; Haltwhistle. I can't get away from it, the centre of Britain ... and gravity.

I tackle the driver. 'What's up? We're in Haltwhistle, aren't we?'

'Ya.'

'Long way round to Birdoswald, isn't it? Look. Here.' I'm pointing at my map.

He looks confused now. 'Sorry, man. See I'm not local. I'm from Scotland. Thought you meant somewhere else – that other place near Housesteads.'

There's a stunning inevitability about this exchange. 'Brocolitia?'

'Ya. That's it.'

This is pantomime time. Here's me supposed to be walking, but not; and now bussing, but I can't even get that right. I can't believe what I'm hearing either. There couldn't be anyone looking or sounding less Scottish than the driver. The Caribbean is written all over him and London's on his lips. What's he doing in Scotland? Then I catch myself thinking it. Why shouldn't he be in Scotland? Why shouldn't he be Scottish even? It's as if I had a stereotype of a Scottish person tucked up in bed, with a wee dram. Of course he's Scottish. What else?

'Ah drive down each day, see.'

'Good way, isn't it?'

'Nah. Only 25 miles.'

'Yes? Is that all?' What an ignoramus I am. I hadn't realised Scotland was so close, but now I'm trying to figure out what to do, while the chap is ready to move off.

'Look. I'll stay on,' I say impulsively, 'for the ride.' But that's ludicrous. I don't know where he's going. I could end up in Scotland. 'Where're you going anyway?'

'Once Brewed, Housesteads, back to Once Brewed, Haltwhistle and the Museum. Ah can drop you off there, if you like.'

'God, no thanks.' Much as I enjoyed the Museum, that'd be the third time.

'What about beyond?' I look at the map.

'Ya? Gilsland's the next stop after.'

'I'll settle for that. Not far from Birdoswald, is it?'

'No. Not if you say so. OK, that'll be another …' I hand over the extra cash with the resigned tut you'd give a wallet that you'd just dropped down the toilet.

LXIV THE PARTITION

If I think I'm in for a relaxing reverie, I have another think coming. I'm the only passenger and, now we've broken the ice, there's nothing my driver wants to do more than chat. He's out of earshot to begin with, so I perch behind him on the front seat. Trouble is there's a partition. It's odd conversing with a disembodied voice. To see what he's saying, I lean round the partition, but have to clutch a rail, to stop myself toppling over.

'I live at Lockerbie,' he says. 'It's not so good really. After the crash, there was a lot of jealousy. Know what I mean? Some claimed stress money and got it. Others left it too late and 'adn't got a penny. And there's petty crime. House prices are cheap though. Ya can still pick up a place for 60 grand. Buy a shed in London, that would.'

'Have you bought yet, then?'

'Nah. Might move. See, wages are low, 'alf London rates, but's less stress and they'm not checking up on ya all the time, if ya's missed out on a stop like.'

'You from London?'

'Ya, ya. Essex, man.'

'What, born there, were you?'

'Ya.'

'Saying you're from Scotland had me wondering.'

'Nah.'

'Do they all ask where you come from?'

'Ya. Essex, that's what I say, man. Always. Sunny Essex.'

We laugh.

It's getting awkward peering round the partition. Even holding on to the rail, I'm sliding off the seat when he goes round left-hand corners. Standing is easier then. So I'm up or down, depending on what the road's doing, how I'm shifting, the gear he's in and what I'm hearing. It's all haphazard – a stupid game – like as a kid when, if they called out one name, you didn't do some action and, if they didn't, you did. Or was it the other way round?

LXV BACK CHAT

We're at Housesteads now and a lady comes running. She wants him to wait a few minutes for the rest of her party.

'Sorry, madam. Gotta schedule to keep.'

She pleads, but he's unmoved or rather has moved, too soon. How could he? He may be a stickler for timekeeping, but hasn't he got time for a touch of humanity? I remember a bus driver in Portugal who didn't dream of driving off till two biddies – one inside and one out – finished their conversation. He had his priorities right. This driver has lost all reason. There won't be any profit on this run. I'm still the only passenger, ears pinned, whether I like it or not.

On the way back now: Once Brewed second time round, Haltwhistle re-gained and, despite the cornering, I'm still hanging on … most words.

'Automatic, this is. Gawd help us; some long distance coaches 'ave 15 gears.'

He used to do coach holidays but that took him away from home too much. Now he just does Euro Disney. 'With a PSV licence, you can.'

I'm getting well geared up on his predispositions. Union man, I should think. He goes by the book. I could put him wise about the soldiers' lot but hesitate. It might sound like point-scoring.

'Family man, are you?'

'Ya. Wife and two kids.'

'With you?'

'Wife, yes. Daughter; she's settled – Dumfries. But son; he's back in Essex. Won't budge, like ma Dad. Tell you what,' he says. 'Ya never wanna teach 'em to drive. Ah tried it with ma daughter. Disastrous, man. She'll never drive again.'

'No?' I say, tightening my grip.

'Nah.' There's a story there. His pause for breath as a giveaway.

The Museum's come and gone, and we're on to West Indian culture. I can see he harks back, from the nostalgia in his voice. He likes the food. Yams and sweet potatoes still fill his plate, and he has a big CD collection of reggae and calypso music. An hour in the company of this chip-chirpy man and I know a lot more about him than he about me. He's asked me nothing, but he'd have told me more, much more, if Gilsland hadn't hove into sight. Me, I haven't walked one inch, but am I tired. It must be the aerobics and ears bent round the partition. I could do with an early night.

LXVI CONFUSING TIME

One decision straight off; I won't make it to Birdoswald. Chicken I may be, but I can't take much more and my feet back me up. I'll wait for the next bus to Banks and the B & B. Besides, I said I'd be there around five and it's a quarter to already. It'll have to be the Hopper again – Hadrian's Wall Bus.

With a certain glitch in travel plans fresh in mind, no one's going to catch the right bus this time more than me. Supposedly, one learns from mistakes. I'm not so sure. A new situation need only be a touch different from the old for one not to make the connection. And this is one of them. The nasty little devil that got me in trouble last time is waiting to pitchfork me again. But I've spotted him. The devil's exactly where you might expect, in the detail on my timetable.

My bus is due at 17.22 opposite the post office, but a bus to the opposite destination is scheduled to arrive at 17.20 also opposite the post office. Ridiculous. How can two buses to opposite destinations arrive on the same side of the road? I smell a rat. Two, in fact. Rat one: if that isn't right, how do I know on which side to wait? Rat two: if that is right, I can still get scuppered. With only two minutes between them, the later bus might arrive first. Let it pass and I'd miss mine, last bus of the day. Oh, and what about rat three? There's no sign of a bus stop.

This is all too confusing. It could be a long walk to a chicken salad. I'm going to check. They should know at the post office. In front of me is a distinguished old gent in a grey suit, a little frail from the sound of his voice. He has to straighten up to speak to the young girl who's serving. She takes a while, not because his wants are great, but because of what he has to relate.

From the bits I'm overhearing, it's the dream he had last night. I'm not so sure I should be privy to this. It's about her. I step back respectfully and pretend to get absorbed in the grocery shelves. When I look up, it's the expression on the assistant's face I read. She doesn't have to speak. Eyebrows raised, eyes sliding to one side and I'm in the picture. She's heard it all before, a dream the dear old gent's reliving every day.

It's put my confusion in context. I don't ramble. My turn and I'm the soul of decisiveness. 'Is that where you wait for the bus to Banks?' I enquire, pointing to the wall opposite.

'Yes.'

'Thanks.'

All the same, I decide to jump out in front of every bus in sight, wherever it's coming from or going, to this side or that, brandishing a placard on which is written in black protest-march letters, 'BUS! STOP!' Well, almost. It'll have to be plan B:

1. I do whatever I must to stop the first bus.
2. I say nothing beginning with 'B' except Banks.
3. I check that the driver is going nowhere near, so forcibly that neither of us is in any doubt as to where he's not going.

Of course, the first bus arrives first and the matter is despatched quicker than it takes to drop a clanger. Well, almost.

'Not going to Banks, are you?'

'It's the one behind, mate.'

'Thanks.'

So obvious that things turn out all right when they do. And I'm so relieved they do that I quite forget to ask why both buses stop on the same side. Hardly an epic survival story, is it? But I never thought that catching the right bus could be so challenging.

LXVII RIGHT WRONGS

Simple pleasures: all it takes is a dash of wholegrain mustard on a chicken salad and I'm back on the road to contentment. Here I am at my Banks B & B, settling into a high-beamed room with views over rolling hills from a balcony. What more could I wish for? Feet up on a comfy sofa, I switch the telly on – first time I've watched since I started this offbeat journey. It's a moment of pure indulgence, but I'm gripped.

With no idea what's coming, I have turned on exactly as Adam Hart-Davis is doing for me *What the Romans Did for Us*. As if that is not enough, there follows a programme on the British Museum's top ten treasures. What else is top of the poll but the Vindolanda writing tablets? It's as though I've tuned into my own special interest channel. I'm half expecting the anchorman to come out with 'and, Laurence, what would you like to see next?'

It's been a day when I've been reminded; how plans can go awry with one slip of the tongue; what heavy weather one can make of getting things right; and how, without even trying, everything once more is on song. How can one be dealt such different hands, one after the other? How could I forget? It's the game I'm playing – a game that's got me guessing.

But why would I want it otherwise? Aren't the most satisfying tales those of the unexpected? Like the bookseller who, seeing a young woman puzzling over a street map, stepped outside to assist. They ended up marrying and now have two kids, directions neither could have anticipated.

There's a maxim at management schools, 'Fail to plan and you plan to fail.' It sounds worthy. Chances are that, had I invested in the right equipment and toughened up my feet, I would have completed my walk as I'd hoped. But I'd be the poorer for that. Ill-prepared plans can prove beneficial. Mine have. And mistakes are good for you. Whether they take you forward or back, you learn something you didn't anticipate. Even losing your way can be productive. It sounds like RULE THREE to me.

LXVIII SETTING UPSET

All this thinking has walked off with my early night and I am persuaded that nothing will put me in the mood for sleep more quickly than a hot shower. I am lucky to have one available en-suite but the nurse's advice still rings in my ears, 'Keep the plasters on for a few days and the feet dry.'

Having inspected the shower, I work out compliance. There is a ledge either side of the tray, wide enough to stand on. If I direct the shower head down centrally, my feet will be nicely clear of the spray. I ought to know better. The unorthodox stance calls up the memory of a short city break in Lisbon a year or two back when I had a very short shower. The shower being over a bath, the hotel provided a grip mat. Seeing a powerful gush from the nozzle, I stepped on, anticipating a good pummel … with good reason.

Suddenly I was on the receiving end of that party trick where the tablecloth is pulled but the table setting isn't. Except that my setting was. I performed my own stunt, the human cascade. My head just missed the edge of the bath before finding the tiled floor, and soon after a lump big enough to remind me to think things through.

But I can distance myself. I see no reason why this shower should end up with any head-banging. I strip off, ready. The shower control looks simple enough; one knob with a central cap which also revolves – a technology I'm sure even I can master. One turn of the knob to the point where the water should be hot and out comes a full spray. I wait a while for it to warm up. It doesn't. OK I figure, the cap must set the temperature, so I turn it too. No difference. But it feels very loose. Does it do anything? Perhaps – and why didn't I think of it before? – it's an electric shower. I rule that out. There's no sign of a pull cord or switch.

Now I am well aware that what seems simple may belie more subtle controls. So I resort to variously pushing and pulling the knob, while revolving it, if you'll pardon the expression. The knob doesn't like this too much, nor does the water temperature which remains obstinately cold, while I don't remain remotely dry.

There must be a fault in the hot water supply I reckon. But it's too late to knock up the management. Besides, I realise one only has to think of a shower to feel most incredibly tired. I dry off and retire, leaving battle lines to be redrawn tomorrow.

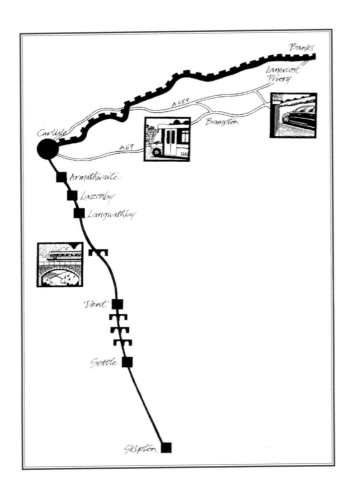

DAY FIVE

*'How will I know whether I'm right to stray so far
from the path?'*

LXIX KEEP GOING

Last night a dream reproached me. I was on board ship, in charge of some emergency warning system. But, with far more interesting pursuits in mind, I kept wandering away. Of course, my absence was soon rumbled. I received a severe dressing- down and was told to stand by my post.

This shirking of responsibility has got to stop. So I stand by the shower and turn the knob again to the point I did yesterday. Out comes the full spray … cold. What possesses me to do so, I haven't a clue, but I continue to turn the knob. Simplicity itself! Before I know it, I am straddling the most incomparably excellent shower, with a streaming jet of water hot enough to put me in the pink.

If anything beats the virtuous feeling of being clean, it has to be the sheer smugness of working this blessed shower in the first place. My next ablutionary challenge, I hereby announce, must be to power-wash my hands after using a public toilet without looking as though I've wet myself.

But before self-satisfaction gets the better of me, let's not overlook one fact. It was the one extra turn of the knob that made all the difference. And the lesson I didn't know I had to learn; persistence pays off. Stop too soon in any endeavour and you'll never know how close you might have been to a breakthrough. Shall we call it RULE FOUR?

Often, a lesson we thought we'd learned comes up again in a guise we don't recognise. This is one such. For my sins I once did door-to-door canvassing. We were monitored by a thick controller who stood at the end of the street to make sure no door went unknocked. And this, despite the fact that we had to record the house numbers on a sheet, the contacts made and result.

'Don't you trust us then?' we'd say innocently.

'Only as far as I can see you,' spoke the professional bully.

The closest we got to a pep talk was 'keep going.' But the real wisdom was, 'It takes fifty knocks to get a lead. Stop at forty

[DAY FIVE]

nine and you'll miss it.' That was double-glazing. He wouldn't have known about sandal-begging. Now that's different. One knock: two pairs.

LXX LONG ROAD

Clean and clear-headed, I'm in an uncommonly good mood at breakfast. I compliment Sandra, the proprietor, on the herbal teas in my room, convinced that any B & B which includes peach & passion fruit in its selection must qualify for an extra star. But the arrival of her other guests, an elderly couple from Durham, puts me in a more contemplative frame of mind.

It is apparent from the way the husband helps his wife to the table that she is infirm and, once seated, he launches into, *'Oh Lord, for those gifts we have received in thy great mercy, and for those we are about to receive through thy good grace, may we be truly thankful.'* I breathe deep, picturing him as an army chaplain while I, a humble foot soldier, fight the good fight. And that better be in God's company.

Strange that I should be so moved by this simple act of thanking the Almighty. We know that breakfast will be received – some of it's already been in my case – but, all the same, it has made me think what thanks I ought to give for what I might receive today. Thankful I am, most of all, to be walking with nothing like the long-term pain this poor lady must endure.

'She's crippled with arthritis, she is,' he says. 'We reckon the damage was done when she worked in the Land Army, planting and weeding on her knees. 34 years ago it started.'

How critical an affliction must be when you keep tabs on its birth date. Since then, she's had to have two new knees.

'Does anything relieve the arthritis?' I ask.

I want to hear from his wife, but he speaks for her. 'Fruit, garlic, broccoli and spinach are all supposed to help but,' and this stuns me, 'we've tried magnotherapy for a month and already she feels relief.' She nods. That's something.

But 34 years? Hard to believe that it's taken this long to find out. Talking of persistence, how doggedly one needs to seek other remedies when conventional medicine hasn't worked. He knows a blacksmith who had knee trouble going back many years and was recommended to tie magnets round his legs before he too found relief.

In this day and age, the right choice of treatment can still hang on word-of-mouth, whether it's drinking hot water for a migraine (from a chat at the bus stop) or applying a packet of frozen peas to a swelling (overheard in a post office).

If only he would let her talk, I think, that would help. If only she would. The man is even monopolising her arthritis. He has to be in charge, so I call him Major for want of a proper name and he doesn't disabuse me.

It may be his age – he retired 15 years ago, at 67, he tells me – but everything about him tends to the dogmatic. When I start talking about computers, he's adamant that he doesn't know and doesn't want to know, but in a curious turn of phrase that is quite endearing, 'I go bonky if I try to take in too much.' Bonkers, sir. Bonkers.

A full breakfast and I'm ready for the off. His parting advice, though, is tinged with reproof, 'A lean horse for a long road.' He makes me feel like an old charger who's snaffled too many oats. That's how I read it. Or have I made too much of what I've taken in?

LXXI DOUBLE TAKES

I want to make Carlisle today, but hobbling all the way is out of the question.

'Why don't you look round Lanercost Priory first?' Sandra suggests. 'I'll run you there if you like and you can catch the bus to Carlisle.'

That's really kind of her, but how is it I'm won over so easily? I ought to be miffed by my willingness, but I'm not. Say 'yes' and 'go with the flow.' That's what Sue said at Twice Brewed. I may be off foot and off track, but let's see where this 'yes' leads.

Change is in the air. Blue skies have bowed to a sullen grey. En route to the Priory, there's a rumble of thunder, but distant. No lightning, not that we see. Sandra drops me at the entrance. I yank my rucksack out of the boot, give thanks for everything and turn towards the Priory when it's me that's struck. I shouldn't get too blasé about coincidences but even if this wasn't I couldn't miss her. Standing at the bus stop is someone I recognise instantly, irreverent that I am, as The Proud Possessor of Twin Treasures.

'Amazing,' I say, 'meeting you again like this, miles further on.'

'Yes. I'm doing a circular walk today from Brampton. The bus will be here soon. It's due at eleven.'

'Oh, I see.'

That's a poser. My first choice worked out well. But which flow do I go with now? I can take my time at the Priory and wait for a later bus, or catch the eleven o'clock one. With twenty minutes to go, there's still the chance of a quick shufti and a chat on the bus. That's it. Best of both worlds.

The church is 12th-century, Augustinian. August is the word. This soaring building is cathedral-like in scale but I love the random mix of pink sandstone and grey limestone. It speaks of human expedience. I might guess where some of it came from and a snatch of conversation confirms it. Hadrian's Wall, of course. Except that there's another twist. After the dissolution of the monasteries, much of that stone went too, as the shells of outer buildings testify. You'll find it in local houses now. Men come and go but the stone from Hadrian's Wall is reincarnated.

I wish I had more time but better get a move on. The bus is due any minute and there's some news to catch up on. Only as we meet up, do I notice two things:

1. The ground I've just covered double quick.
2. The hobbling – it's hardly hurt.

The tablets are working. So are the socks. So are the sandals. Praise be.

LXXII PAST PREOCCUPATIONS

On board the friendly Hopper, we wind the windows down on our experiences. My account is full of gusts, hers quietly contained.

'No more finds on the path,' she tells me. But, visiting a quarry, she came across the wedge marks made by Roman masons when they start splitting the stone. I can see how engaged she is by the discovery. It's all down to her keen eyes and you'd have to know what you were looking for. Most people would pass by without a second thought. Yet you hardly need a leap of imagination for those marks to take you right back to beginnings and the masons' skills, without which no frontier could have been established.

'They used a pick to dress the stone,' she says. 'It's double-sided and curves to a sharp edge both ends.'

The sheer scale of the industry required for this enterprise is mind-boggling. Not just the fetching, selecting and building bemoaned of by Abraham. But winning the stone and dressing each and every one by hand in the first place, to make up the mammoth four million tons of stone, clay and mortar that went into Hadrian's Wall. How many working hours of how many days, in how many weeks, months and years of a man's life were wedded to stone? Do we hear his voice when we follow the Path? We ought to.

In her spare time, my amateur archaeologist organises walks for up to thirty people but what depresses her is their talk – about what was on telly last night, and usually the goings-on in Corrie.

'How can they,' she complains, 'when they're missing out on so much else?'

'I know. I've met people like that; oblivious to what's around them. You'd think they'd leave the telly at home, wouldn't you?'

'And not smoke, while they're walking. And what do you make of this?' she says. 'I work with the less able but I don't know what to do about one of the young blokes. He's absolutely fixated on The Beatles, spends his whole life on the Internet finding out whatever he can about them, down to the minutest detail.'

'At least he's got an interest, you could say.'

'But he's got a life to live and he's living it through them,' she protests.

'Yes. You'd have to ask why and what's missing, that the Beatles mean so much?'

'I hope I can find out.'

'He has a choice, doesn't he? Not like those masons.'

'But he doesn't want to take it and that's sad.'

Our conversation's cut short. A pity. Her stop's coming up. She's off and still I don't know her name. But I do know her all the better for the work she does and the dilemmas she confronts. And for that she is, without doubt, a treasure.

LXXIII OBSESSION SESSION

So what if an interest turns into an obsession? What could she do about it? I wasn't much help, was I? But, no sooner has she gone than I start coming up with ideas. Typical.

When I was at school, one form teacher grew tired of hearing about the top ten. 'Is that all you can talk about?' he'd say. He didn't bang on about it but had his own answer. He gave me a set of long-playing records and the lively character of Elgar's *Enigma Variations* did a great job of opening my eyes ... and ears. One generous gesture works wonders. No accident that, years later, I chose to live on the edge of the Malvern Hills, in the heart of Elgar country.

That might be a pointer. Perhaps she could introduce him to other musical genres. He's bound to know that George Harrison got caught up with Ravi Shankar. Why not start him off with a CD of Indian sitar music? He might even latch on to other cultures.

What about sharing her enthusiasm for the Romans? Or, better still; let him get his own sense of history on one of her walks. Then again, he might get hooked on walking. And where would that take him? I dread to think. But, as long as it's not a cul-de-sac, an obsession needn't be bad. It might lead one on, or live happily with others.

A cousin of mine springs to mind. His partner was heavily into pottery, so the front room housed the kiln. They both loved pets, so the kitchen doubled as a menagerie. His hobby was making posters and the first floor was home for his silkscreen set-up. I can't remember how bedrooms fitted into the scheme, but you had to go up to the very top floor to watch telly. That seems the right priority. You'd have to go out of your way to see Coronation Street. Well, there's an answer to that dilemma too.

But it's easy to be glib with solutions, when other people don't even think there's a problem. It's like asking the chap who keeps a cow in his back garden and takes it for a walk down the High Street each morning, why? When he's ready to move on, he will. So I'll leave them there and enjoy the rest of the ride.

LXXIV THE SPLASHDOWN

Off the bus and I'm ready for whatever Carlisle can throw at me. It does. Spots of rain are dotting the pavement. I fumble for my makeshift protection, an old cycling waterproof that only ratchets up my identity crisis. Am I a bussing walker or a bikeless cyclist? Anorakerish, either way.

But a small, fussy-looking woman finds me approachable. 'Rain's come early, 'ant it?' she says. 'Who shall we blame, love? I know, Tony Blair.'

Sharp up here, aren't they. Even the weather's politicised.

My first stop is the Tourist Information Centre where they find me a room at East View Guest House. I'm happy about that. My last B & B was South View and it feels right working my way round the compass. I might as well check in now, since Tony Blair is courting more unpopularity. Dots are being joined by dashes, then splashes.

But I'm bemused. I pass by a terraced house with a front border of worn out busy Lizzies that a man is watering … in the rain. I stop, look up pointedly to the soggy heavens, then down to his hosepipe but say nothing. He gets my drift.

'Ee, you can never tell up 'ere,' he says.

I can tell by the damp feeling down my neck that my waterproof isn't.

'So what's it going to do this afternoon?' I say, defying his beliefs.

'It'll be showers, probably light, but clearing,' comes the definitive answer.

'Good, because I'm going to Settle on the train.'

'Yes?' he says. 'Scenic ride that, but not much there. Church, pubs. Why don't you pay a bit more and go on to Skipton? Plenty to look at. Canal and bookshops. Nice town, it is. I should know. I'm a tour guide.'

'Well I never. Yes. OK. Thanks.'

I settle on Skipton immediately. Funny, but already I'm feeling at home … in Carlisle.

LXXV LOCATION? LOCATION?

Julie, it is, who takes me to my room past a row of straw hats looking distinctly unseasonal on the stairwell wall. It's a single at the top of the house, light, airy and reasonable. Only £20.

'Ideal,' I say, 'and en suite too. The shower … um … not difficult, is it?'

'Not at all. Just remember to switch the electric on.'

'Yes, of course. No problem. This'll suit me fine.'

I ask her about Carlisle. 'Oh, this is Cumbria,' she says, obliquely.

'I didn't know. I've only just arrived,' I say, confused, 'but I'm ignorant on counties.'

'I'm not from here, you see. I'm from Yorkshire. We've not long moved.'

Where you come from: it matters, I can tell. Where you're going too.

'Ah ... right. Well, I'm planning to visit Skipton this afternoon. What do you think?'

'Oh yes. Nice ... very nice,' she says. 'But why don't you go a bit further? Now Haworth, that's interesting, the Brontes' place. One long street, soaked in history. And there's the museum.'

'Yes? Thanks for that.' Going with the flow is one thing, but where does it stop? It's a flow too far, Haworth. Sorry Brontes. I'll have to call a halt at Skipton. I'll find out when I get there whether I'm right. 'Oh, while I think about it, you wouldn't have a polythene bag I could borrow, would you?'

'I've never been asked that before.'

'It's just that I don't want to hump the rucksack about.'

'I expect I can find you one. Will Debenhams do?'

'Yes. Champion.'

I'm not proud. I'd have taken Asda, Tesco, even Marks & Sparks. She wouldn't know, of course. It's not so much for carrying as for more immediate damp-proofing, up top. The feet? Well, you can't get wetter than wet, my old Dad used to say.

LXXVI TRUMPET BLOWING

I've picked up my ticket for the 14.26 to Skipton. Busy Lizzie man was right. The rain has scuttled off, the sun is peeking through and I am heading back to the Tourist Information Centre to thank the young lady for fixing up such an agreeable guest house.

True, she was only doing her job, but why should that stop me? I'm sure the Major would agree on that and it all comes back to you. Talking of which, a gratifying dryness is already infiltrating the damp.

So even before I reach the Tourist Centre, I'm feeling happier. Thinking the thanking must have helped. Want to cheer yourself up? Thank someone. That's got to be an appreciative RULE FIVE.

But there's more. Ahead of me and crystal clear, the sublime melody of Schubert's *Ave Maria* is soaring above the hustle and shopping bustle of the city street. It's a trumpet call I can't resist.

There's something about brass instruments played in the open. My father loved playing the trombone – for Lawrence of Arabia once, on board ship to Mespot (as he then called Mesopotamia – now part of Iraq). I never heard him play. Losing his teeth before I arrived on the scene, he lacked the embouchure he needed. But the tingling has come through. Other people have stopped in their tracks to sit and listen, as if they've been caught by an overwhelming need to rest. I have to take it in too but on the only seat that's left, under a tree, next to some pigeon droppings.

Not at all down-at-heel, our busker looks every part the professional, with a neatly lettered sign, *John Barker, Magic Trumpeter* in front of him, as he works his way through an eclectic repertoire. One man is moved to walk from the opposite side of the street to drop coins in an open case. Another man's head jerks from left to right shoulder. Nodding off doesn't come easy on a bench but arms fold contentedly over a beer belly, while the strains of 'No matter what …' break over him.

What with the dancing shadows of the trees around, the rich smell of new ground coffee and the singing trumpet, it's a feast for the senses. And so beguiling that I might have missed this other moment; a little girl springing a joyful skip and jump, as she passes the trumpeter with her mum. It says everything about the magic that this music is weaving. Adults may feel, but a child shows it.

It's two o'clock. I'm sorry to go. My thanks earn me a bonus smile at the Tourist Centre and, heading back to the railway station, I come across yet more buskers serenading the shoppers of Carlisle. The streets are alive with the sound … but cities shouldn't simply tolerate; they should positively encourage. How about a festival of busking, Carlisle? You'd be the ideal city to celebrate the unique contribution they make to the street scene. I'd come back for it.

LXXVII SIGHTSEEING TRIP

A fellow walker says, 'Don't miss the Carlisle-Settle line.' A busy Lizzie waterer says, 'Go further' and I take that on board too. But as the Arriva train slips out of Carlisle station in its blue and green livery, I'm stumped to know why. A nice view hardly stacks up as a reason, especially with my feet on the mend and seeing if something turns up sounds pathetic.

When other diversions have arisen, I've gone along with them. But isn't this blatant self-deception? What could possibly justify it? And how will I know whether I'm right to stray so far from the Path? All I can do is sit back and see what new twists there might be to this game.

Here's one for a start. You can open windows on this train. But the young chap in front can't. He's pulling his sideways.

'Perhaps I can help.'

He accepts my offer and, with one sharp downward tug, fresh air streams in.

'There you go.'

'Oh, I thought you had to pull it out,' he says, 'not down.' He looks a bit abashed, though I'm not sure whether the reddening is sunburn on his freckled face or embarrassment.

I know how he feels. His window catch could so easily be mine. How is it one idea gets fixed in one's head? Perhaps he's only been exposed to windows that open out.

Grasshopper that I am, my attention is captured by the evocative names of the stations. Wouldn't you want to take up arms and go thwacking in Armathwaite? On the other hand, I'd be content to loll about and let bygones be gone in Lazonby. Even more so in Langwathby, where I picture myself lying in the bath, languidly watching the world go by. Which is, more or less, what I seem to be doing right now.

LXXVIII SCALING HEIGHTS

Forty minutes out of Carlisle and the stage is set for change. Town and village give way to cottage and farmhouse. An hour out and we're right on the moors. Run-off from the peaks has cut scar-faced channels. Running up and across hillsides, stone walls define man's hold on the land but, without definite courses, that looks tenuous. Not the grip of a Hadrian. Dips are deepening. Heights are heightening. A viaduct crosses a valley and man is dwarfed.

Far below, a cameo scene is enacted at the side of the road by a tiny knot of figures. A car has careered down an embankment and stopped short of a tree. A fire engine is attending. I can imagine how perturbed the car driver is as he explains.

'This stupid bugger comes speeding round the bend, right in the middle of the road. I had to swerve. Next thing I knew, I'd toppled over the edge. And no, he didn't stop.'

Then there is the matter-of-fact expertise of the fireman. 'We get two a week like this, sir. It happens all too often on these narrow stretches. It's people who don't know the roads – foreigners and such. Bad luck you met him here. Could've been worse though. At least you didn't crash.'

I bet that isn't much consolation to the driver. But a few months on, his hurt feelings will have healed. In a week or two, the fireman's memory will be nothing but an entry in a log. In a few seconds, a distant witness is travelling on and any contretemps I may have had with the world has been scaled down by a grandstand view of another's.

That's what hills do, like the Ais Gill summit we've just passed. They put problems in perspective. Soon we're pulling into the highest main line station in England, at 1150 feet above sea level and I'm smiling. Only someone with a huge sense of humour can have called it 'Dent'. Or perhaps with a real sense of scale.

LXXIX THE SIGN

We're rolling through dramatic scenery now, viaduct after viaduct commanding views over the Dales and beyond, in great sweeps, towards the spine of England, the Pennines. These are views that ought to be enough to validate this trip. Instead, my eyes focus on more telling details; the bands of hikers trudging along paths that I can only wish to tread. Theirs is an intimate relationship with these wild spaces; mine a flirtation.

In less than half an hour, I'm stepping out at Skipton. It's a flat reception. The station is a good way from town and any hope of a pleasant saunter is vanishing as fast as the grey blanket overhead gathers gloom. 'Ee, you can never tell up 'ere' has never seemed more certain.

Soon after I start walking, the first spots spatter. I'm a dark green waterproof now that's hustling along the pavement, topped by a Debenhams' designer rain hat, shielding sandalled feet from the worst of the dollops.

A decision has to be taken fast; shelter. A shop doorway does for a minute, enough for me to discover a hunger. It's a dash to find an eatery that will do but there's one that might, on the other side of a bridge, on the left; a fish and chip café.

One look and I know with absolute certainty, this is it. Ahead of me is a sign that leaves no doubt. It's not that I've hit upon a National Award-winning Fish and Chippy, which I have. It's simply the name: 'Bizzie Lizzies'.

LXXX BIZZIE LIZZIES

'Cod and chips, with mushy peas and a cuppa please.' It comes to a modest £3.85, and no extra to eat a few steps down in the café section which, glory be, looks out on the canal – the Liverpool to Leeds Ship Canal. It should be a peaceful scene but I'm still buzzing.

Is this it? Is this why I've come? To discover a dubious link

'Is this why I've come?'

between a man watering busy Lizzies – the very one who tells me to go on to Skipton – and an eponymous Fish and Chippy? Preposterous.

The rain is sluicing down the parapet of the bridge, splashing a neat demarcation line in the canal where open water meets the arch. It's a frontier; feverish eruptions this side; a calm reach beyond.

A stately procession glides by. It's a flotilla; a pair of adult swans sailing under the arch, with five adolescent cygnets in tow. Long necks. Wide bodies. How such dissimilar components make up such graceful forms, I wouldn't begin to know. But what's really bugging me is a whole concatenation of events: not just this one, but all the other fancy-bumpings-into-you-again. How do they fit in?

A man is puffing his way along the towpath, shoes slopping and all the more soaked for his slow rate of knots. He reaches the sanctuary of the arch and, propped against the back wall, wipes his brow with a crumpled handkerchief before pulling his trousers over a flapping shirt tail and tucking himself in.

With a mouthful of mushy peas, I play consequences. Just suppose a young woman appeared from the opposite direction and sought refuge under the bridge too. What if they spoke? And what if this sparked off something life-changing? Well, he'd bless the bridge and the downpour that brought them together, wouldn't he?

The seven swans return from their sortie and cruise past. The puffer collects his breath and sets off again. The moment that might have been is gone. But wait a minute. There's something here I've missed. He'd forget all about getting wet. That meeting, if it happened, would put it out of mind and make it right … as rain. How could I not have seen? That's what I've taken my chance encounters to mean. It's not coincidences in themselves; it's what they tell me – that I'm going right, that I'm on the right track. RULE SIX, if ever there was one. Marooned by No.178 Belmont Bridge, I'm as close as I can get to an epiphany and all I needed: 'Bizzie Lizzies' Fish and Chippy.

LXXXI CHANGED VIEWPOINT

It's a revelation I want to commemorate and three women sitting at the next table give me the opportunity. 'Excuse me, ladies, but I wonder whether one of you would mind taking a photograph.'

I've already sorted out in my mind what I want; me sitting down, with the bridge in the background. Symbolic, I think.

One of the ladies jumps up. 'Yes. I'll do it.'

I hand her the camera. But no. She won't have it; my idea.

'I'm taking the photo,' she insists. 'This is better. You stand over there.'

She wants to point the other way, looking back along the towpath and won't take no for an answer. She's wielding my throwaway camera like a sharpshooter. I'm reminded of the indomitable women of Haltwhistle. With the matriarchy in these parts, the boot's definitely not on my foot. I acquiesce.

'Well yes. Of course. Will this be all right?' Click. I'm shot. Never mind. I live to tell the tale.

The worst of the storm has passed, but the force of it was enough to breach the window seals on the *Dalesman* canal boat moored in front of us. Water has pooled on a table and a young chap mops up before the next trip.

My time's short. The two hours I had in Skipton have all but gone and I can hardly do other than flit into one bookshop before sidestepping the puddles on my way back to the station. It is laughable what little I've seen of the town. I'm sure there's so much more. But I do know why I've come and for that I feel amply satisfied. And well fed.

LXXXII FEELINGS UNSEEN

To see more of the views on the return journey, I bag a window seat on the other side. But how is it I manage to get distracted? I have discovered an unusual talent. I confess it. I spy. I can look people in the face without them knowing. Or, to be more precise, a woman in the group of seats beyond. Or, even more precisely, her reflection in the glass.

This is quite a novelty. These days, looking someone in the face is not far short of assault. It's bad enough being stared at in the mirror at the barber's while he puts me through the third degree on my musical tastes, estate agents and the penal system. I have to be careful what I say. My haircuts nearly always end up being political. But to stare at someone else for no reason: that's something new. This is a rare opportunity not to be arrested for terrorism.

The woman I'm looking at I'd put in her forties. Silver flecked hair, pencil-thin features and a cultured sort of Joan Bakewell face suggest considered opinions and civilised appetites. Classical music lover, I'd say. Probably an opera buff.

But while I'm engaged in this character assessment, I'm aware of a disturbance. On the other side of the carriage, opposite her, are three young blokes. I can only see two clearly. One I typecast as a swarthy Italian with Latin looks and locks, and black leather jacket. Another, facing him, has long blond tresses. When he turns round (and it is he), I catch a glimpse of a fresh, innocent face that you'd never suspect of malevolence.

The two of them are having a bit of a ding-dong. First, it's harmless banter, then insults and swearing before it turns ugly. The Italian produces a wet towel – so they've been swimming – which he starts flicking at The Innocent, who retaliates with another wet towel, which is then joined by a third. Now a flicking, effing and blinding war has broken out.

I'm a spectator, caught in a split-screen struggle between the towel fight and the taut expression of the woman, sitting uncomfortably close to the conflict. Up to then, she'd been looking out of the window rather dreamily, enjoying the view but is now positively discriminating in its favour with all this hoo-ha.

It must be alarming for her, wondering whether the aggro will spill over. There's only one thing she can do and I'm not surprised: close eyes. It's not tiredness. She's shut it out but she'd have to cover her ears to blot out the obscenities. What does she make of all this? Look as I might, I can only guess. That's shut away too.

Deliverance. The fracas comes to a sudden end. The Italian has taken a direct hit in one eye and, boy, it looks painful. He stops flicking straight away and rubs it over and over, turning his head this way and that. It's gone strangely quiet. No one asks if he's all right. It looks callous.

Not long after they leave and, when we reach Carlisle, I realise how their altercation has taken me over. Ask what I've seen. I won't even mention the view.

LXXXIII BACK OFF

The voyeur in me aroused, I muscle in even more on my walk back to the guest house. They're changing films at the Lonsdale Cinema. Letters are being removed, one by one, from the display panel. One film title is in transition.

'I can't see *Nic.olas Nick....* pulling them in,' is my flippant remark.

'No. It doesn't make a lot of difference either way,' says the man on the ladder.

Candid in Carlisle then. I wander on, full of speculation that *Nic..... Nick....* might have just finished showing.

Next it's an estate agent. A couple of retirement age are looking in the window, at the hair-raising prices, no doubt. Remembering the bonny bus driver's words, I breeze over their shoulders with, 'You can still buy a decent house in Scotland for 60 grand, you know.'

'But who wants to live *there*?' comes the retort. 'You've got to pay over the odds to live in England.'

Oops. I am suddenly reminded about Border Issues.

Enough excitement for one day. A quiet night is in order, and what better way to sign off than a soothing shower? No trouble with this one. Power supply on, one turn of the knob and it's all systems 'go'. The warmth of healing waters is balm to my overactive mind. I soak it up. There is but one sacrifice: the plasters come off.

Now I'm ready to step out but there's a hitch. When I turn the knob to the 'off' position, the shower goes cold and doesn't stop. Can I believe it? I can't turn this one off. I turn it to warm and off again. Still it stays on. Ridiculous. Unless I jump out of the way each time, I get a cold dousing. Aha … never let it be said I'm a slow learner. Next attempt and I keep turning. Swoosh, dribble, phut. Off it goes. But only at a full 45 degrees beyond the 'off' mark.

It's enough to destroy one's confidence in language, not keeping up as it isn't with shower control systems. One 'off' is certainly not on. There needs to be a sliding 'off' scale. I have some suggestions.

Here's how my scale goes:
1. Nothing like 'off'.
2. Coming 'off'.
3. Going 'off'
4. Pretty well 'off'.
5. Quite badly 'off'.
6. Only just hanging on 'off'.

And then there is the decisive turn to the ultimate finishing line: written 'off'. It must be time to retire.

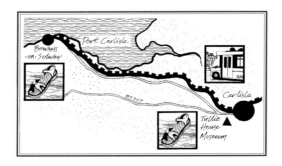

DAY SIX

'There's no disguising it: I don't know what I'm doing.'

LXXXIV VEILED APPEARANCE

Morning has dawned and with it a drip-drip of doubt, from wet pavements outside and from the 'ruddy big hole' in one foot that's still weeping. I make do with a strip of the old plaster. What I can't patch up is the gaping hole in my plans. I should be walking to Bowness today but Skipton has changed all that. It's taking me in a different direction, though I can't figure where. The only compass is the one in my stomach that points to breakfast.

Two tables are already occupied by foreign visitors. A volley of glottal stops ricochets round the room but it's the silence from one corner that draws my attention. Seated at a table facing the wall is a lone woman, staring in front, never turning round. She seems overdressed in full-length black coat, heavy denim jeans and with long straggly hair that looks, I have to say, unwashed.

Her breakfast's finished, all but sips from a cup. The only time I hear her speak, it's an abrupt 'No thanks', as if an offer of more toast is an insult. When she gets up to go, I'm in for a shock. Where from the back I'd guessed thirties, her face is in its fifties. Soon after, I pass her in the hallway. She's settling up. 'Mistake,' she says. 'I've left the keys in my room.' Strange woman.

I can often sort out situations in the loo but, instead of thinking out a strategy for today, distract myself with a silly game I use to while away those waiting hours. I look for a word, preferably short, on a packet or bottle, then see how many other words I can permutate using at least three letters. It's *Olive* I've settled on, and here goes: *Love* ...*Live* ...*Lie* ...*Oil* ...*Vole* ... *Vile* ... *Veil* ... *Vie* ... *Voile* (what a find) ... and *Evil*. I rule out *Olé* as a foreigner. Perhaps I shouldn't. But what a mixed bag.

There's *Oil* in *Olive*. Interesting. *Love* and *Live Vie* with *Vile* and *Evil*, while *Lie* and *Veil* are embedded suspiciously and I suppose the *Veil* could be made of *Voile*. Where the *Vole* fits in, I haven't a clue. Has he gone to earth?

But all this nonsense has done the trick. Taking my mind off the decision has helped me make it. I like Carlisle. I already knew. So I'll stay and catch the last bus I can to Bowness. Not walking, no. Mistaken? Maybe. But it's what stares me in the face. And wasn't that Rule One? Julie agrees I can collect my stuff later.

There's dampness in the air but the rain has eased as this neophyte steps out, thirsty for enlightenment. I don't have long to wait. On passing a surgery, the thought occurs to me, why not pop in?

'There's a bit of a queue for the doctor,' advises the receptionist. OK, but perhaps she can answer my question.

'Yes, of course,' she says. 'The antibiotics *would* be doing that.' And it's obvious, when I think about it. They're driving infection out. Let them get on with the weeping.

While she's putting me wise, a little boy plays with a model farm layout in a children's corner. He's planning the farm track for the animals, placing cows, erecting gates, siting a barn and all the time burbling away happily, his thoughts in the open. I'm in the surgery. He's out on the farm.

LXXXV ALL RIGHT?

I'm heading into town, about to cross a street. There's a figure standing in front at the same junction: someone I know just from the back – I should do – the lone woman at the breakfast table. And even if I hadn't recognised her, I would have taken notice. She's talking into thin air. I can't make out what she's saying but I don't have to hear to guess she's disturbed.

She's complaining and that's no surprise. The woman is loaded up to the gunnels, with a suitcase on wheels, a heavy backpack and yet another bag she's carrying. Does she need help? The least I can do is say something. What comes out is a paltry, 'All right?'

She rounds on me. 'You ask if I'm all right? I worry about that. Why you ask? I tell you if I wasn't. Now pees off.' And even louder: 'Pees OFF.'

'All right. All right.' All wrong. I walk on, quickly, away. And why wouldn't she tell me off? I knew her by sight, but she didn't know me from Adam. Naïve of me, wasn't it, to imagine I can go up to any woman in the street and say, 'All right?' I should have known better. You don't do that sort of thing. Not these days.

Ignorant that I was, I deserved the rebuke. What I accepted in a child as normal earlier, in her I deemed disturbed. That's perverse. Most of us talk to ourselves at some time. I save my worst vitriol for myself. 'You crumbling edifice, you pile of poo' are mild when I can't find my car keys, to look for specs I think I've left ... in the car.

Except, there *was* a difference. The boy babbled on about his farm as if he owned it and I might curse a memory lapse today. But her soliloquy was surely rooted in the past. Really, there was nothing I *could* do. Carry a bag? Useless. What someone's been through, what they can't let go, that's heaviest.

Now I bear a burden. Walking into town, oblivious to all else, I can't dismiss it. Being told to 'piss off' is the very thing I cling on to. Perhaps I needed to know. It shows how the bad sticks. A blunt RULE SEVEN, that.

In a haze of self-reproach, I continue past the railway station and alight on a noticeboard outside a building, the Citadel. It advertises a courtroom reconstruction, staged for tourists. But, blast, I've just missed it and there's no one in attendance. I'm tempted to gatecrash through an inside door, were it not for the absurdity that dawns on me, of an offender breaking and entering a court scene. 'It's all right, yer honour, I only wondered what it was like to be in the dock.' But I already know. Can I let myself off with a caution?

LXXXVI WALL WHISPERS

There's no disguising it; I don't know what I'm doing. I'm back to what stares me in the face; the time I need of the

Bowness bus. And who better to tell me than the Tourist Centre not far ahead? So that's soon sorted – and where to board it – leaving me a few hours to spare.

I leaf through their literature. Carlisle has links with some famous figures; from the elusive King Arthur, a reputed early ruler; through Mary, Queen of Scots, incarcerated at Carlisle Castle; Henry VIII, who ordered the Citadel's construction; to Sir Walter Raleigh, married in the Cathedral. A rich history here, but I can't connect. The Citadel escaped me and I'm not in a castle or cathedral mood.

What else can I do? There's nothing particular going on this afternoon. 'How about Tullie House Museum and Art Gallery?' they suggest. 'It's only a short walk.'

'Yes. Of course.' I'd read about it somewhere and I'm a sucker for museums. Once inside, the contents are like my favourite sweets, liquorice allsorts. It's tempting to snaffle the lot. But that can be deadening. Instead, I prefer to dip in and surprise myself with treasures I'm sure to come across. One of those chewy blue ones would go down well, right now.

There's plenty to entice me at Tullie House on three floors, not least a whole area devoted to the Romans and Hadrian's Wall. Perfect. But, saving that for later, I start at the bottom, in the Millennium Gallery on the lower ground floor. Dallying in the minerals section, I can't ignore a monumental exhibit beyond. I'm intrigued. It's called *The Whispering Wall*.

A Glasgow-based artist, Stephen Skrynka, has had a 30m long wall built entirely in glass blocks, about 30 of which, spaced high and low at random, each contain a recording of someone's observations. Within each block is a pair of spectacles, symbolising the owner's personal view of what he or she has seen. All you do is put your ear to one of these blocks to activate a play-back. How inspired. I'm entertained by the very idea.

LXXXVII THE EAVESDROPPING

At first, I'm inclined to work my way along, listening to each in turn. But that's far too straightforward, not at all like me. Then there's a moment of déjà vu. The last time I had that thought, I was into a spot of sandal-begging. This isn't knocking on doors though and it's not that I know what I'm begging. But, if I dodge about eavesdropping, maybe I'll find out. My feet come to a stop. Try here? Why not? I stoop.

'You've got to look for the beauty, otherwise you just see desecration. Some people you look in the eye and see nothing. Others might be compassionate, sly or distrusting. When you cannot trust anyone, that's very sad.'

Yes, yes, I want to answer. That sounds like the odd woman. But here's the solution: play up the good – A RIDER TO RULE SEVEN. It's the good one forgets. There's a message for me there. Turn up the trumpet and pipe down the 'piss off.' I'm encouraged. Further on, my step falters. I bend forward, ear at the ready.

'It was two in the morning,' a female voice says. *'I was smelling acrid smoke and bonfires burning. There was nothing where a row of houses had been, a shocking sight, like the aftermath of a blitz.'* She was a reporter who covered the Lockerbie story. But who also saw children playing by a river and remembers commenting, *'She's caught her first trout. She's bubbling and smiling.'*

Remarkable that someone, who might well have closed in on the death and devastation, opened up to a child's innocent pleasure. I move a few paces along. Should I go further? No. This will do. Listen.

A chap is talking about how differently witnesses see the same incident. Bizarre. That Lockerbie account showed how people's impressions are coloured by the way they look. He wonders what witnesses can possibly agree on. *'What did the offender do?*

How did he do it? And were his trousers yellow or light brown?'

My mind goes back to the towel fight on the train. What did I think they were up to? Best mates having a bit of a laugh? A disagreement that got out of hand? Or deep-seated animosity? I couldn't even agree with me. I walk on, then come to another instinctive halt.

This speaker is a tonic. *'I go out without an umbrella, not expecting it to rain.'* That's his philosophy. He was once entertained by the improbable sight of a bloke with a shed balanced on a bike. Unshakeable optimism, that. What can you not do, if 'not doing' hasn't entered your head? RULE EIGHT, I nominate. But I need to get *my* head around what I've heard. It must be time for a break.

LXXXVIII THE SOUP

They have a mighty fine Garden Restaurant at Tullie House and there's nothing so fine as broccoli and Stilton soup to help me take stock. *'The Whispering Wall'* experience was uncanny. *'You've got to look for the beauty,'* the first voice declared, hot on the heels of my being 'pissed off' and, to reinforce the point, the reporter who might have seen only devastation found hope. *'We all see things differently,'* commented the next speaker before the last chap proved how much. He always looked on the bright side.

Bit of a coincidence, isn't it, that all four views connect. But what do I read into it? That I should take a new look at what I'm doing? I thought I was. But then, hardly have I deserted one wall than I'm walking past another.

Straining after a purpose is getting me nowhere. Perhaps I should stop looking. The hardest thing, it seems, is to just do. There, at least I get another rule out of it – RULE NINE – and prove the point admirably. We always have to find reasons for what we're doing. Well, I do. That's plain stupid. It's as if I need to be working towards a degree in diversionary tactics to justify what I'm up to. Come to that, it's like asking why I enjoy this soup when it's all gone and I'm scraping the sides for more.

Time to move on. The Romans beckon but, as I step up to the first floor, there's a commotion: bloodcurdling shouts rend the air. I can't hear the words, only the horror. There are simulated flames and flashes. A building is on fire. Someone's home is being torched.

This dramatic audio-visual display highlights a chapter in British history I've never heard of. For over 350 years apparently, from the early 14th century, the Borders were wracked by vicious feuds between some 200 families; the Elliotts, Armstrongs, Maxwells and Grahams among the most menacing. The Border Reivers, as they were called, made an area known as The Debateable Lands ungovernable, not least because, in slipping across the border and declaring themselves English or Scottish as it suited, they escaped justice for their brutality.

It's unimaginable, the nightly fear of a family that armed raiders might sweep down from the hills, spring a surprise attack and make off with the sheep and cattle, destroying their home and leaving them for dead. Without knowing, we hark back to the Reivers' depredations every time we mourn. It's in the language. But what a sacrifice, and to bequeath us one word: 'bereaved.' It's about as strong a pronouncement of loss as one could utter. There can be no harsher threat than that to a whole life and livelihood. And no greater uncertainty than not knowing whether you'll survive the night.

LXXXIX UNHOLY ORDERS

Not for the Roman soldier the life-threatening anarchy of the Reivers. His was a much more ordered existence. But reading contemporary accounts in the Roman section, I can appreciate the hardships that regime might impose. One writer,

Juvenal, describes a son as being 'centurion bait, his brains half-cudgelled out whenever he leaned on his spade.'

The strict discipline, intensive training and numerous fatigues must have left their mark, while the northern climate tested endurance. The historian, Tacitus, relates an occasion when 'The whole army was kept under canvas, though the winter was so severe that ice had to be removed and ground dug before tents could be pitched.'

Distractions of drink and the bathhouse, with the chance to lay a few bets on the back of a game, were welcome relief from the rigours and routines of dawn-to-dusk workdays.

But the soldier had dreams like the rest of us. High on his list, no doubt, was to meet the right woman, have children, marry after his 25 years' service was up and citizenship granted. In unguarded moments, he'd be cultivating his own plot of land. He might drift into sowing spelt (*triticum spelta*, an old form of wheat shown in a display case) from which to bake bread, decorating it with seeds from poppies (*papaver somniferum*). Perhaps he'd transport himself to a family repast, dipping into a bowl of olives picked from his own tree and quaffing a good, strong, vintage wine. But, for all that, his dreams might be in vain. Having signed on in his late teens or early twenties, and with an average life expectancy of 40, he'd be unlikely to outlive his time in the army.

So where could he turn for a hope of better times to come? All round me is evidence of a huge support network; a whole pantheon of gods. Bordering the Wall, temples were built and altars set up (of which many examples are displayed) for libations using flagons or shallow bronze bowls (*paterae*).

The gods ranged from the king of them all, Jupiter; through a soldier's god Mars Thincsus; to such as Fortuna, the goddess of good luck, complete with horn of plenty. She'd have my vote. He could call on gods co-opted from other countries, like Mithras, the god of light from Persia or the Assyrian goddess of love and war, Astarte. Handy having a foot in both camps. Even local gods were embraced. I like that. If you don't have a god that fits the bill, call on someone else's, off-the-peg.

But just when I'm beginning to applaud this overture to ecumenism, I'm brought to earth. A pity, but someone cobbled together a 'god' of imperial discipline, with altars to remind soldiers that any orders or punishments had 'divine' backing. I bet that rankled. I can imagine a humble auxiliary coming up with a choice substitute for 'divine.'

' "Conniving swine" will do nicely. Pass me the chisel.'

'Certainly, Vitriolus.'

XC TURNING POINT

I ought to be heading for the exit. My time is flying, but I'm stalled, as if missing something I haven't found. It would help if I knew what it was. Then I remember. There's a word for it. Weird what the mind dredges up. I'm at a bus stop and this American girl is telling me about a Portuguese word that has no English equivalent, *saudades*.

'It's a kind of yearning for the future,' she says. And why don't we have it? – I might have asked. But if that's what I have, it's back to the future because I've decided what I need. Another whisper. I can't resist one last eavesdrop at the Wall.

Trusting my feet will guide me again, I stop when there's no impulse to go on and bend an ear to the nearest glass block. A man is talking about a time when he was in a low state. Six foot tall and on heroin, he was down to six stone. *'It sounds dramatic,'* he says, *'but I could see every bone in my face, like a skull.'* He was surprised to wake up some mornings. *'Some mornings, you wished you hadn't.'* Then, *'one terrible morning, I woke up to hear John Lennon was killed. I had to make a decision: live or die? I knew, if I went back to London, I'd go back on.'* So he decided to stay where he was, in a Warwick Road B & B.

He describes his efforts to come off heroin, to reduce and reduce, collecting his giro cheque every week, *'hibernating,'* he says, until one day *'a woman came into the B & B whom I married two years later.'*

And it stops. It stops. At the very point I'm panting to hear more, the recording ends. I can't contain myself. It sounds like a turning point. Did he win through? I can't leave it, on the edge of knowing. 'Excuse me,' I ask the attendant, 'I've just been to the Wall. There was a man talking about his struggle to come off heroin. What happened? Have you any idea?'

'Oh yes. I know him,' she says. 'He was mayor for a short time.'

'Yes? That's great.'

'He used to go round, giving talks to young people, warning them of the dangers.'

'Brilliant. With his experience, he must have got through to them.'

'I'm sure he did. But, you know what? I think the pushers should be targeted more,' she says, 'not just the dealers. It's them who get the kids hooked.'

'Yes, of course,' I say, appreciating her good sense but thinking, thank God it worked out so well for him and what a relief not to be left hanging in mid-air.

Tullie House has been kind to me. En route to the guest house, I turn into my B & B road. I thought it rang a bell. It's Warwick Road, the same as his.

XCI OPINION POLLING

Back at East View, I return the Debenhams bag and settle up, but I'm still curious about the odd woman. I ask Julie, ' Did you notice anything ... sort of different?'

'Not really. She wanted an omelette on top of a full breakfast.'

Well, that's not earth-shattering. 'Nothing else?'

'Her suitcase was very heavy but she was going on to the Lake District, so she'd need more clothes.'

'That's all then?'

'All I can think of.'

'I see.'

I hump up my rucksack and bid goodbye as Julie hurries to answer the phone. In the hallway, the visitors' book lies open. I pause – might as well sign off – but, pen poised, my eyes stray. I waver over one entry. There. Isn't that her? 'Magda Windsor'. It has to be. The other names are foreign. Her address though? She's given it as Carlisle Road, London. That can't be right. Dubious, coming from me, but it's a coincidence too far. She's pulling the wool, putting down the first thing she thought of. Her name's probably made up too.

There's an irritable twitch of leg on my way to the bus station. Set against the drug-addict-come-good story, hers is a closed book. I'd hoped to flesh out my impressions. I haven't. Julie didn't even think her odd. She was, wasn't she? OK, forget the thinking-out-loud bit, but she had let herself go and staring at walls isn't normal. She *had* to have hang-ups. Look how suspicious she was when I spoke, as though I'd threatened her. And now she's in hiding. Isn't that enough?

Enough? What *am* I thinking? What am I *doing*: trying to prove she's odd? Speak to her once, a couple of fleeting glimpses and the ink's hardly dry on the certificate. If anyone's hung up, it's me. Or should be. You'd not think I'd heard about 'looking differently'. It takes more than a whispering wall; a loudhailer from an open-top bus more like, blaring out, 'She's not suspicious, but streetwise; not hung-up, but getting on with life like you should be, opinionated git.'

That says it. Who am I to judge? How would I know what makes Magda, or whoever she is, tick? And why speculate? Does it help? Certainly not her. Nor me. See what happens when I do: I get a feeling, form an opinion, thrash about for corroboration and when I don't find it, I'm peeved. I want her to fit my misconception. It's insidious. And so is the pressure to keep producing pigeonholes. Try not to, when The Office Gradgrind asks, 'What do you make of so-and-so?'

'Oh, I haven't a clue,' you say.

'What? Haven't you noticed? She writes dates back to front ... dyslexic. She wears black lipstick ... Gothic. She's got hairy legs ... hobbit. Are you brain-dead or something?'

No. Call me ambivalent, but I know where I am: sitting on the fence.

XCII BUTT ENDS

Actually ... on a bench at the bus station, waiting for the number 93 bus. And there's a hunched-up woman at the other end, taking a long drag on a cigarette. A short while ago, a short, stubbly chap made a beeline for her and said something I didn't catch. When she replied, he erupted. All I heard was a good dose of the verbals and his saying what sounded like, 'You always ... .' before he stormed off.

She looks pretty downcast now in a legs-crossed huddle, puffing at the pavement. I can hardly believe I'm not saying something – well, anything – but certainly not, 'All right?'

It's a fine line, knowing when to open your mouth or button up. Too late now. The moment's passed and I'm left wondering what it was all about. My first thought: he was cadging cash, probably to feed a drug habit. But that's a ready-made pigeonhole, lifted straight from the addict's story.

Might there be another scenario? If he did say, 'You always ...', he must have known her. Could he have been her son? Maybe I was in at the tail end of an argument that started way before. Suppose she'd just visited him. He'd poured her a mug of tea and she made a harmless remark like, 'Forgotten I take two sugars, haven't you, son?' That's how it begins. Enough to trigger off, 'What d'you expect? It's been such a long time' from him.

One thing leads to another. Before long, he's asking what sort of mother leaves her little boy with the drunken arsehole of a father. And she's spitting, 'Don't you ever speak to me like that,' before seeing herself to the door.

He's left stewing. But there's hope in second thoughts. He tracks her down at the bus station. 'Look, Mum, I didn't mean to drag that in. Can't we talk it over?'

She kills him dead. 'No. You don't want this old woman around you any more.'

He loses his rag. 'Suit yourself then. You always did.' She clams shut. He steams off.

Was that how it went? It's all very well my making a mini-soap out of people's lives but there she is, taking a last few drags, having to live it. What's she thinking? – 'I only wanted to make it up to him?' She stubs out the cigarette on the bench, drops the butt on the ground and shuffles off.

She's not heading for a bus though. It's the street. Where is she going? I could be tempted to follow, were not my bus due any minute. There's no next episode for me. On the edge of my seat, I've no choice but to let go.

XCIII BOUNDARY SHIFTING

Hopping on the number 93, I'm struck with a thought so utterly banal that I can't believe I'm thinking it: after I left the bench, I boarded the bus. Until I did, I couldn't. I'm laughing at the sheer imbecility of doing otherwise. 'Excuse me, driver, but I've brought my own seat with me.'

As the bus gets going, it's obvious: moving on means leaving something behind. But certainly not the RULE TEN that such an astonishing revelation demands. That 'something' might be a seat, but a situation too, like the bench-end one. I'm at home with this versatile concept. A comforting conviction is settling over me that, until I left one path, I couldn't hope to find another.

Now that we've cleared Carlisle, the view is opening up to the Solway Firth. Those hump-backed convulsions that the builders of Hadrian's Wall had to contend with have given way to a sprawling plain of rough pasture. But, flat as it is, I can see no sign of the Wall. Instead, there's that most natural of boundaries between land and sea – the shore – a line not held fast, but ever re-defined by the turn of tide and whim of wind.

A boundary like that keeps you on your toes. After all my sidestepping, it's one I can identify with. But that's precisely the point, isn't it? My boundary has changed. 'The Whispering Wall' should have shown me, but I hadn't seen. Of course there is more than one way of looking. My feet might have walked one boundary but, on this new one, it was attitudes that had to shift. It's holding on to them that builds the boundaries between us. The 'odd' woman opinion I clung to was a classic case. She did me a favour. I had to see things from the other side.

How long has it taken me to get here! Perhaps I shouldn't feel too bad. It took the Romans nearly 300 years to change their viewpoint and move on. They had to: there were other borders to defend. I'm different. I had to move on to find out where I'd been. Better tack that on to RULE TEN.

As we approach Bowness, I have mixed feelings. I might know what turn my 'walk' had taken but the end of the road is in sight and that's a shame. There's scant time to exercise this two-sided mind and, now that I've alighted from the bus, the one-track version soon kicks in. A board outside The Kings Arms promises that superb meal I was alerted to back on the Wall, but only from six o'clock. So I book in, win a bright, comfy single room, offload my rucksack and distract my stomach with a walk through the village.

Weeping no longer, at least my sandalled feet are on message and I'm free to focus on the straggle of cottages and modern infilling. Except that much of what I think I'm seeing is the stone from Hadrian's Wall. Half-truth, no doubt. And ...ah, of course ... there's always another way of looking. If stone which built a barrier becomes a welcome home, isn't that a good thing? I probe the curtains for signs of life. TVs flicker. But then again, where are the bookshelves? Aha ... too cosy and those walls spring a trap. What does it take to shake people out of the familiar chit-

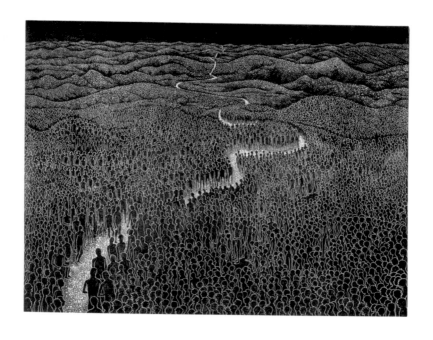

'… it was attitudes that had to shift. It's holding on to them
that builds the boundaries between us.'

chat and flat-on-your-back screens? Perhaps a spell of hostel life, rubbing shoulders, like the Romans did in barracks. The same group of eight or so men in sleeping quarters: that would wake up a few attitudes.

Then I wake up. I'm at it again, pontificating. And here's a timely reminder of what I've come to, a dog's bottom. A model, in fact, in a garden, engagingly real. There is only a back end with tail ahoist. But I can picture the front burrowing, frisking a hole far below. And the passion, anticipating something unexpected or maybe turning up a bone buried earlier. It's all there in that backside. Every lawn should have one.

XCIV TIDELINE TREASURE

A little further down the road, a path leads to the coastline. Under a clear, blue sky, the Solway Firth stretches way out to the Irish Sea. But when I reach water's edge, my eyes are on the ground, a confused mix of tussocky grass and gravelly inlets. This one is strewn with the bric-a-brac of stone, bleached wood, odd shells and, dare I mention it, a glint of something faintly archaeological. I rush over and pick it up. No good. Not Samian, even I can see. It's a triangular shard of salt glazed ware. Pity.

I keep looking though. There … what's that? A slip of terracotta juts out. I winkle it up. More promising: a sliver of once-fired clay with a streak of black oxide, hand-brushed perhaps. But again, no. It's splintering, too reminiscent of the laminating roof tiles on old barns.

What next? You never know. I can't forget the time my daughter and I stumbled across an alien on the beach. Two doleful, marshmallow eyes drooped from a dome of translucent flesh, about a foot and a half across. From the purple-frilled dome, eight great tentacles splayed out, tinged pinky brown. OK, it was some species of jellyfish unknown to us, but crossed with a fashion-conscious octopus for sure, with Brit-Art pretensions.

This is more like it. I'm perusing a chunky pottery fragment, about one inch thick, in the mud. It's rounded, like the rim on a weighty earthenware pot. I wipe my thumb over the surface of … what? An amphora? But there's a slight sheen to both sides and it's thicker than a museum specimen I've seen. Another thought finally puts the boot in: the sleeve of an underground drain.

Never mind. Despite the spent adrenalin, I'm still holding my finds. And that's the wonder. I'm not hurling them back. Why not? Well, it's too easy to overlook the other way of looking. The feeling's lingering that, until afterthoughts cut in, these were treasures. I want to latch on to that first look, full of possibilities and give it a life. Yes. I shall keep all three, and mounted in a cabinet, of course, complete with inscription.

How will it read? *Never forget what might have been?* That sounds a bit sad, looking back. *Hold on to the first look?* Still not good enough. Too much of the 'hanging on.' Better a light touch, something like, *Let be what might be?* Yes, but a little long. I play with the words. *Let be what might? Let what might be.* That's more like it. I repeat it like a mantra, changing the stress each time, working to a rousing crescendo on the final *be.* RULE ELEVEN declaimed. And there's no one around to even think I'm … well … odd.

Time to return, but I'm detained. On the foreshore, half a green bottle with a domed base is sparkling in the early evening sun, the one bold colour statement on this stretch of beach. It warrants a wider audience. Back in the main street, a perfect podium presents itself; the top of a stone wall by the bus stop. Who will see what I have seen? I position it carefully to show the glint to best advantage. There. That's a thick enough slice of two-sided thinking to go on with.

XCV LAST COURSE

Within sniffing distance of the sea, it has to be fish. Besides it's Friday, so breaded haddock, salad, chips and peas do me fine. There are only two of us in the dining room. An elderly lady has finished her meal and she's querying the bill.

'£7.90,' she says, 'for the meal and sweet? Have you charged me for the wine?'

'Oh yes,' the waitress confirms.

'You're sure? Very well.'

'Reasonable, isn't it,' I note, after she's settled up. When did I last hear someone question a bill because it seemed cheap?

'Yes. If I'd known about this place, I'd have stayed here, instead of up the road.'

'I was lucky. I heard about it on the Wall.'

'You've been walking the Path then?'

'Off and on.'

'Alone?'

'Yes. And you're by yourself?'

'Most of my friends have died and, of those left, none seem to want to keep up with the Romans. But I had to come to Bowness.'

'Good for you. Your first time, is it?'

'It is.'

'And mine.'

The waitress is asking if I want a sweet. I surprise myself. 'No thanks. That was so filling. Perfect.'

Then the lady asks if I know how far it is to the sea.

'I've walked one way,' I tell her. 'It only took a few minutes. Are you thinking of going?'

'If I can make it with my feet.'

'I know how you feel. Well, I fancy the other direction. We can take it slowly. What do you think?'

She may be a little unsteady, but this lady's held herself together. She still has a trim figure, her eyes are sharp and, when she speaks, every word is precise. You want to listen to what she says. A walking companion is a novelty and I know I'm in for some sprightly conversation.

'So what's your interest in the Romans?' I ask, as we amble down the road.

She smiles. 'I can hardly remember not being interested. I used to take school parties from Gateshead and Middlesbrough along the Wall. We talked of charabancs then, not coaches. My husband was head of one of the camp schools, which ran from February to November. We had to cope with 200 children at a time, every two weeks. They kept us busy, but I loved it.'

'I bet there wasn't much you couldn't tell them about the Wall.'

'I wouldn't say that. You know, Hadrian gets the credit but his legate, the British governor, Aulus Platorius Nepos, was responsible for its building.'

She wants to set the record straight. 'Perhaps you can tell me from your experience something I've been wondering: how do you know whether you're seeing Roman stone?'

'It's not easy. The facing stones tend to be tapered, though you wouldn't know from the front. If the stone is scored, with a kind of serrated groove, it's likely to be Roman, but that's when they keyed it ready for plastering. And, in any case, the stone weathers.'

'It must do, but I know it gets re-used. Have you seen any in the village?'

'There's one wall I've spotted that may have some. It's not just wall stone. Sometimes bits of altars were built in. But don't forget, there was a turf wall first this end and, even after it was reconstructed, the sea could have swallowed much of the stone.'

'Of course. I should have realised.'

'What about you? What brings you here?'

'You mightn't believe it. But for a trip to New York, I wouldn't be here now.' I tell her about the woman in the Metropolitan Museum who never liked Caracalla. 'Hard to credit that he arranged the murder of his own brother, joint emperor, in the presence of their mother. And to think they called the enemy barbarians.'

'Then you might be interested in this,' she says. 'In the crypt of the abbey church at Hexham, there's a stone with the name Geta scratched out.'

'I tell her about the woman ... who never liked Caracalla.'

'Really? I know he tried to obliterate all memory of his brother. Anyone who had as much as written him a letter was killed. Thousands died. I must see that stone sometime. It's a lasting condemnation, that missing word.'

'When you do, you have to go along a passage to the far end. And be sure to look up, or you could miss it. It's in the ceiling.'

'How on earth did it get *there*?'

'Well, the original church was built mainly of Roman stone from Corbridge, a major garrison and supply town. That's where it came from.'

'I see.' More re-cycling. 'Of course, it's easy to forget all the emperors that had charge of the Wall after Hadrian, like Caracalla, some … what? … 70 years on. He came over first with his brother when their father, Septimius Severus, was emperor. They tried to push into Scotland but skirmishes by northern tribes wore them down and they had to fall back on Hadrian's Wall.' I've a feeling that she's well aware of this, but she listens politely as we round a bend.

'Oh dear,' she says, 'my feet. I'm not going to make it. I am 86, you know.'

'I'd never have guessed,' I say, and I wouldn't.

'You'll be all right, walking back?'

'Oh yes. I'll manage. Maybe I'll try again tomorrow. And bring a good book.'

'OK. I've enjoyed our little talk. Good luck.'

She turns to go when, for once, I remember, 'I must ask you your name.'

She looks round, suddenly intent. 'I'm a Tait,' she says and, with relish, 'Scottish by inclination, but English when it suits.'

Can that mean … ? I'm thinking only one thing. 'What? Not a reiver?'

'Through my husband, yes.'

The Reivers again! I only hear about them today and here I am bumping into one of the families, still looking both ways. And proud of it.

If she'd managed a few more steps, she'd be with me now on this bench overlooking the sea, towards which the sun, in full-blown gold, is slipping. The few sounds only point up the silence. A collared dove coo-croos in a nearby tree. Among staunch thistle heads, long grass stalks swish. And the tide's in no rush. Waves shuffle on shore, before beating an apologetic retreat.

We met. We parted. And what to show for our exchanges? No whoop of surprise surprisingly, more a nonchalance. It's laughable, after everything – the coincidence: hitting upon an 86 year old lady, with years of walking Hadrian's Wall, but coming to the end of it like me, for the first time, alone. And so clued up on the Romans that she knows about an obscure stone with a name scratched out, embedded in the ceiling of a crypt. Who else knows that? And harking back to what started me off. And then, to cap it all, I ask her name. I remember. Surprise isn't in it.

But there's a noise, the revving of an engine. A bus is pulling on to the rough ground behind and, before my mind can get back on track, the driver climbs out of her cab and walks towards me.

'Hallo,' she says. 'Not waiting, are you?'

'No, no. Just watching the tide come in.'

'Oh. This is my three-minute nicotine stop,' she says, lighting up.

'You probably need it,' I say, 'what with those narrow lanes and reversings.'

'Yes. I was down to do Carlisle today, but the driver didn't show up for this run, so they put me on instead.'

'Bit irksome, eh?'

'Not really. I'm pleased. It makes a change from the traffic, especially on a Friday.'

'I suppose it does.'

With her puffing and our small talk, three minutes soon elapse.

But the interruption is welcome. I can embrace change too. While she negotiates a three-four-five point turn, my thoughts take a different direction.

Benches and I have had a long and happy association. In my twenties, as a rookie copywriter, I took time out every lunch hour to sit on a street bench. I learned more what makes humanity tick there than sitting in any office. Single mum's stories, a nun's tale once, the epic lives of shopping bag ladies – all gleaned from bench-side chats. One day, a diminutive rag-and-bone man who was his own donkey, pulling a cart, told me how proud he was of his five strapping sons. The paradox that is mankind registered with me even then. But the unexpected always catches one unprepared, unless one keeps in training. Worth a RULE TWELVE, surely.

Perhaps I ought to extend an open invitation. If I sit here long enough, who else might beat a path to this bench? A long-lost relation? An old classmate? Not impossible, given time. A Roman centurion then? Now that would be pushing my luck. Well, how about … aha … a reiver? Not so far-fetched, is it? But see how close one might … not get. If her feet hold up, she could be here tomorrow. But I won't. The facts are: if I hadn't eaten when I did, if she hadn't queried the bill, if I hadn't opened my mouth, nowt would've come out. If, if … where does it end? I can look all ways and be no closer to knowing how paths coincide, or how we connect. But then, I don't have to understand communication technology to answer the phone.

With a last look at the wisps of cloud skirting the sun, I retrace my steps. Two girls are playing on swings in a front garden. 'Hallo,' one of them chirps up, in mid-swing. I 'Hallo' back and, for no particular reason, their greeting is enough to set me off. It's as much as this playmate can do not to hop and skip all the way back.

Just as well I don't or I might have missed the framed diagram on this side of the pub. It's a layout of the Roman fort – the last one on Hadrian's Wall and the second largest (seven acres, as I recollect). And, something I hadn't realised: it used to be here. The Kings Arms is on the very site of the fort. Tonight I could be sleeping over the commanding officer's quarters. There's a thought.

Now that I know I'll be walking in the footprint of the fort, I decide on a final recce down a back street. A chap is digging his garden.

'Found anything?'

He knows what I'm getting at. 'Nothing,' he says. 'When we moved in, we shifted a load of earth, dug as deep as we could. We thought the house was built over the East Gateway but now we guess a ditch.'

'Pity about that.'

'Yes. They carried out a trial dig in the fields beyond but we never heard what came of it.'

Few traces, if any, remain of this once major fort, it seems. At the end of my 'walk', the past has all but disappeared. It's the present I'm left with. And, with a few drinks to see me off, the rest of the evening helps me forget even that.

THE RETURN

'The box wasn't neat. Nor was my walk.'

XCVII PARTY PIECE

God. It's five to eight when I wake. Five minutes to breakfast and I'm not even up. Fast forwarding, I skim through this cliffhanger with some toothpaste slavering, hap-slappy flannelling and skid-slop shaving. Socks inside out or outside in, I fly downstairs, tails just about tucked in but half tucked up in bed. It may be only two minutes past when I arrive at the table but I'm not ready for anything. My head is whirlybirding. I've had one night of dreams and whatever's fluttering up there, locked in some room, is battering at the windows to get out.

You work back from the last memory, they say. What comes first is a party, full of young things. The music is thumping. There's dancing. We're all having fun and I'm in high spirits, when someone drops a cloth over my face. It has a peephole, so I play along with the charade. Watching without being seen suits me and there was too much to take in before. Now I can focus.

Two partygoers look familiar. They remind me of the girls on the swings. That's it: before the celebrations, we were in a family's mid-terrace house. No mum around and the dad has six children to cope with. They're a handful.

'Do they help you?' I ask.

'It's getting them to eat that's the trouble,' he complains.

'Try peas,' I suggest.

'That's no good. They explode them in the microwave.'

Naughty, naughty but lovely kids. All the time, the place has to be readied for the party. But everything's in chaos; there are workmen in the kitchen; a socket is being wired by an electrician; a plumber's making connections. It's mayhem.

The scene flashes to a carpenter. I've no idea where he slots into the sequence, but he's put together a wooden box. Where do I get the impression from that it's for me? Embarrassing: when I look closer, I see that it's not at all well made. He improvised. It's sub-divided and some compartments which should be the same size aren't. He's mixed up different woods – every one at odds with the next – and even used MDF. With another compartment, he's cut more corners. Instead of four walls, it's roughly hollowed out of something like a balsa wood block. As if that isn't bad enough, the whole box isn't even square. I've never seen such a lash-up. But he's proud of it and I don't like to say anything. There is one saving grace. The lid fits.

I reproach myself for this disaster. At least to have specified the same wood throughout, that would have made sense. Why didn't I think? But then, how could I? You can't choose what someone else gives.

'Don't you eat cereals?' the waitress breaks in.

I haven't even seen the packets. 'Me? Oh yes,' I mumble, miles away. 'Leave off,' I might have added. 'That was some party.'

There are other people in the room and they are hardly real.

'Do you want your certificates now?' I hear the landlord ask two chaps who've finished breakfast. That jogs my memory. A certificate is issued to those who walk the complete Wall Path, having collected stamped proofs on the way. Great idea. Except I haven't. And I haven't.

'Any blisters?' I enquire hopefully.

'No. Only sore feet.'

I try to sound knowledgeable. 'You must have good boots then.'

'Yes. Proper walking boots. Cost £110. That's what you've got to pay for a decent pair,' one of them lets on. I spare them news of my bargain buy.

XCVIII BORDER LINES

Off they go, mission accomplished. And what am I left with? Scrambled egg, tomatoes and a peculiar box, not well made, not even square, that I can't get out of my head. It takes me back to an early Christmas present, a jack-in-the-box my father lavished time on. Sadly, the shock of a highly sprung figure bursting open the lid was too much for that little kid. I cried my eyes out.

This other box is almost as unexpected but, if the walk's taught me anything, it's that surprise makes sense. It wakes you up. You have to make sense of a surprise and I don't need a dream analyst. The box wasn't neat. Nor was my walk. There were hollowed-out times when I was blistered, bothered, bewildered. I had cheap MDF moments, dealing in market banter and Bart Simpson socks, lobbing the wheel and looking for a fiver. But well-seasoned hardwood was there too: Roman sites, museums and the timeless friendship of people I met. How can I forget Geoff and Eileen, my sandal-providers? All had their part to play in this oddly-boxed game. And it hasn't finished yet.

A quick look at my watch. The Carlisle bus is not due till after ten. It's a relief to slow down. There's time for a last slice of toast. After some leisurely packing, I head out greeted by sea mist thinly disguised as drizzle.

Some hikers are already at the bus stop chatting away, oblivious of what stares me in the face; half a green bottle standing on the wall. What did I expect? A flower in it? But I'd hardly know what they'd seen or thought unless they said. Even so, I'm sure the talk would run along the lines, 'Pity kids have got nothing better to do' or, 'Careless, leaving that there. You could cut yourself.'

And why *would* they think otherwise? It's presumptuous of me to imagine they'd see what I'd seen. Besides, the sparkle of green isn't much in evidence today and sharp edges glistening in the rain don't cut it. A caption reading, 'Open air sculpture. Do not touch' won't inspire a discussion of deconstructivism in modern art either. No. I'm being provocative. A broken bottle is too much in the face; too potent an image to be other than what it is. A broken bottle it will always remain, unless someone exhibits it in an art gallery or consigns it to the rubbish dump. But then, a box is a box unless it's a journey. And a bus is a bus is a bus, until it takes you somewhere you weren't going.

When the number 93 pulls up at 10.20, dead on time, I take the destination for granted. In fact, on the way back, I'm hardly being where I am. I'm floating in my own thought balloon, pumped up with memories I don't want to leave behind. The only jolt is when a big, bustling woman steps on board. Taking one look at the company of hikers, she announces mischievously, 'I feel like an intruder without a rucksack,' but with nonconformism flooding her face.

Back at Carlisle, the local brand of humour carries me along. A white van passes with 'Fred Bear Carpets' blazoned on its side. But do his tongue-in-cheek customers have a leg to stand on when their worn out carpets arrive? Of course. You can trust a man who doesn't take himself too seriously.

Other local specialities entertain me in the window of a baker's shop; butteries – a type of scone, I would think – going for 12p, and bridies – meat pasties – for 60p. I have to try one of those, if only for the name. We must shake hands. Trifling encounters maybe, but all serving to remind me I'm leaving border country, where differences taste good.

XCIX ALL CHANGE

I'm aboard the Virgin Voyager and it's 12.01. Talk of a voyage and I'm transported to a steam packet somewhere in the South China Seas but Tamworth where I pick up my connection, that's not on the map. No mention of it over the public address. Tamworth's vanished from the Virgin vocabulary as surely as air-conditioning. If I'm not losing my cool from one, it's the other. I search out the train manager. He'll know. 'Sorry,' he says, not sounding very. 'There's been a derailment.'

'Why didn't anyone say?'

'Sorry, but you'll have to change at Birmingham … um, or Crewe.' He doesn't know which. Now *I'm* feeling sorry. I decide to bail out at Crewe, but abandoning ship isn't easy. The young woman in front can't open the door. No handle. No notice. No escape drill. And nearly, no Crewe. But that's one thing I'm good at, openings. 'You have to pull down the window and turn the handle outside.' We burst out like over-excited popcorn.

I hustle to an information point. 'Wait for the 15.15, direct to Exeter,' the informer says. 'Oh, wait a minute; you'll miss the last train to Barnstaple. No. Go to Birmingham New Street instead.' Surreal. It's all change: Birmingham *and* Crewe. 'You want the 14.20.'

'But it's 14.20 now.'

'So it is.'

Cripes. I run like a demented Rottweiler. Mercy. It's still there to sink my teeth in. At 14.21, as we lurch off, I howl approval for all late-leaving trains.

The ticket inspector is quite pally. 'I'm from Ilfracombe,' he says and, 'Nanny lives there, doesn't she,' to the small boy trailing behind. 'You'll need platform 2A, the 15.42.' Brilliant. We're on terms again and, on common ground with one's fellow man, an air of conviviality breaks out. Suddenly I'm living someone else's life: the woman's opposite. She wants to unburden herself. I'll do.

'What a rush. I've had to collect stock from another branch.'

'Yes?' She manages a W.H.Smith station outlet, apparently.

'It's manic. You can't get people to work Sundays, so I have to stand in and there's the early shifts. Start at five a.m., they do.'

'Tough, eh?'

'I'll say. Then there's my husband. Made redundant, he was. He's had to take a factory job, but that's shift work too. We hardly see each other.'

'Not much of a life, by the sound of it?'

'No. We're hoping by the time we're 55 we will.'

'What? See each other?'

'Yes. We've no children thankfully.'

'You must have some time off though. Holidays?'

'Oh, motorbiking, that's our thing. We're going to the Ardennes this year and the tunnel's thrown in.'

'That's good.'

'Yes. Each year we do a package. We went to Gran Canaria last year. Great time that was: five star. Been to California too.

We wanted to do the Grand Canyon on a Harley.'

'That must be something.'

'But was it hot.' She mimes perspiration. 'And d'you know how much rental they charge?' She doesn't wait for my estimate. '£100 a day.'

'Gosh. So how'd it go?'

'We weren't paying that.'

'So you didn't go?'

'No.'

But soon she has to, getting off at Stafford and when she's gone I give thanks. She's left a can of lemonade behind. I hadn't realised how thirsty I've become. But the '55' business sticks. What sort of progress is this? If they have to wait that long, is their lot all that different from the Roman soldiers?

At Birmingham New Street, it's no different. Platform 2A? No way. It's 12B, they announce. 15.42? Not exactly. More like 16.05. And the connection to Barnstaple, last train of the day? It looks as though I can whistle goodbye to that.

'We're carrying out a survey,' an out-of-breath woman gabbles over my shoulder on the train, as if it's the news I've been waiting for. 'Would you mind?'

'Me? No. Not at all,' I answer, on the hop. What timing! And I'm a sucker for surveys, inventing a new lifestyle for myself, like reading *The Independent* every day instead of the *Daily Mail* or snowboarding instead of gardening. And there's a free pen. But when I read what I've written about the Virgin service , it doesn't sound like the me I'd thought to be. It's so mild-mannered.

They want my opinion about a proposed new scheme next. Now I can let rip. I can't believe what I'm reading. How would customers feel about having their luggage collected from home and delivered to their destination? Separately indeed! It's to save space on the trains. This must be Planet Mush. No, I plead. On my knees, I beg you, Virgin. Don't, please. Please, don't. The thought of all that luggage arriving after you've left or leaving before you've arrived, to moon around in some Virgin cyberspace: it's more than I can take … or is it? Look at it from the other side. Losing luggage might be no bad thing. Think of the benefits of this new service: 'We help you realise what you can do without.'

I like it. Virgin, I've changed my mind. I forgive. If you put me on the right platform, that's something. If the train arrives, well that's all right. If it's on time, that might be a bonus … or not. If it's going where I am, all well and good … perhaps. But, if not, *great*. I'll have jumped on board anyway. And, if I end up somewhere I hadn't even thought of, that might be just the place.

C RIGHT PLACE

I might not end up anywhere I'd thought, in truth, if this return trip is anything to go by. But with Virgin's help, I'm getting used to the unexpected. We make a good team, playing with times, routes and destinations. Everything's borderline on this journey and, if it comes to missing the last train, I could almost feel at home.

In fact, it's hard to escape one last rule – a rogue rule this is, to turn any game on its head – that wherever you are is the right place. Coming up trumps with sandals is one thing, but chop and change trains can be spot-on too. In this game, you win even if you can't see your way to the finish. It would have to be RULE THIRTEEN.

Virgin keeps us guessing. We don't know until we get there: at Exeter, they've laid on taxis to Barnstaple, to round off the voyage. That's fine. If they commandeered a ship of the desert, I'd settle for it. But, for one woman, the shifting sands are intolerable. She puts up a fight. She won't have it. 'This isn't the first time this has happened.' Once is too often. She doesn't see why she has to suffer car-sickness and, worse, being cooped up in the back. 'I bought a *rail* ticket,' she insists.

There's a stand-off. I feel like sticking up for poor Virgin – they're doing their best – but, unsure of my peacemaking credentials, leave the station chaps to deliberate in a corner of the waiting room. The outcome is a piece of arbitration that ACAS would be proud of. 'How about if we sit you in front by the driver?'

'You promise?'

'Certainly, madam.'

The deal's done. That's sorted: her in the front and four fellow travellers in the back, second-class. Two Liverpudlians carry on a running banter to my left, leaving me far behind. The other, a teenage girl, in the little seat facing the rear, retreats to a Walkman.

The road is developing a mind of its own: chicanery I call it, bend after bend. We're shifting too; left after right, right after left, and back again. I fear for the car-sick woman. How is she faring? She and the taxi driver seem to be hitting it off. Perhaps the chatting has helped her forget any queasiness. I try to home in on odd words – not easy above the roar from the Kop end – when one pointed comment breaks through, as touching in its restraint as it is stunning to my ears.

'This is no Roman road, is it?'

No, I shout out ... quietly so that no one hears ... but it's the road I'm on, thanks to the Romans.

Appendix One

BOUNDARY CHALLENGE – or *Ludus finis provocatorii*

THE RULES

1. The first step counts, the one that stares you in the face.
   Take it again and again and nothing can hold you back.
2. Act on your feelings. Don't think too much, if you want to find yourself
   where you feel you belong.
3. Mistakes are good for you. Whether they take you forward or back, you
   learn something you didn't anticipate.
4. Persistence pays off. Stop too soon in any endeavour and you'll never
   know how close you were to a breakthrough.
5. Thank someone. Thinking 'thanks' can cheer you up too.
6. Coincidences tell you you're on the right track.
7. The bad sticks, so play up the good.
8. What can you not do, if 'not doing' hasn't entered your head.
9. Just do. You don't have to justify what you're doing.
10. Moving on means leaving something behind. Sometimes you have to
    move on, to find out what it was.
11. Let what might be. The first look matters, full of possibilities. Give it a
    life.
12. The unexpected catches you unprepared, unless you keep in training.
    Extend an open invitation.
13. Wherever you are is the right place, so you win even if you can't see
    your way to the finish.

   Footnote: In my 'Boundary Challenge' those were the rules I came up with. But if
   you're playing, it will be your rules, of course, not mine.

Appendix Two

I am indebted to Latin scholar Peter George for setting out the translation
options of '*Boundary Challenge*' so lucidly. However, the responsibility for the
final version of *Ludus finis provocatorii* in Appendix One is mine. Specious as
they might be, my reasons for selecting each word were as follows:
   Ludus – I favoured the original *Ludus* in *Ludus latrunculorum*, the Soldier's
Game, and liked the notion that a 'game' might be construed as a 'school'.
   Finis – Since I did want 'boundary' to bear a metaphorical connotation, *finis*
seemed more appropriate than the visual *marginis*. *Finis* also conveyed the

finality that any boundary tends to evoke.

Provocatorii – Equally, boundaries provoke transgression, inviting trespassers and calling attitudes into the open. *Provocatorii* had the right ring to it.

Here then is Peter George's exposition, commenting on my original choice of *Ludus marginis provocandum* and of interest I feel in its own right.

1. The latin of *Ludus marginis provocandum*

In dog English 'A game of a boundary being challenged' might be *Ludus marginis provocandae* or *provocandi* (genitive of the gerundive, agreeing with *marginis*, which can be of either gender).

'A game of a boundary which is challenging' might be *Ludus marginis provocatoriae* or *provocatorii* except that:

(a) The connotations of *margo* are similar to those of the English 'rim' and 'hem' and its uses, both basic and extended, are distinctly visual. Metaphorical notions of 'boundary' are normally conveyed by *finis*, occasionally by *limes*.

(b) *Provocare* likewise is not quite the right word; it retains strongly the original and literal notion of 'calling (someone) into the open' for a fight or some kind of competitive activity.

(c) *Ludus* also means 'school' and *ludus marginis* would perhaps suggest a sewing class where nice young ladies learned how to put purple borders on togas. The way to avoid such ambiguity is to use the form *lusus* instead.

What a Roman would make of any combination of *ludus, margo* and *provocare*, God only knows.

2. Any solution?

Not really; the whole notion of being challenged by inanimate or abstract entities seems rather foreign to the Roman way of seeing matters. One approach might be to cut out the 'challenge' element and simply say: *Lusus de finibus*, which is grammatically acceptable in a heading or a motto.

The closest parallel to the idea that I can think of in *real* Latin is in *Virgil, Aeneid III*, where Aeneas describes his landfall at Carthage as *longarum (haec) meta viarum*,' (this is) the turning point of a long journey'. The concept is both literal (*meta* is the boundary-marker indicating the turning-point in a race and Aeneas, having travelled south-west now turns north-east) and metaphorical in that he has found civilisation and believes his troubles to be over (the fool!).

Index to Itinerary

Index to Wood Engravings by Hilary Paynter

About the Author

LAURENCE SHELLEY left school with a love of poetry and a huge wish to write. But his first job, writing blurbs for a 6'7" senior copywriter, made him feel rather small. Life drawing classes and chats on street benches persuaded him to teach art. Clay caught his imagination though and for many years he taught ceramics at secondary and adult education levels.

There followed spells selling double glazing, gardening and printing business cards. Then he ran a garden centre buildings site before setting up his own conservatory business. It took long enough for him to realise that he had qualified as a Master of Diversions and what he really wanted to do was ... write.

He has contributed poems to many anthologies since and written articles but 'Off-the-Wall Walking' is his first book. Its theme could only be how diversions can transform any journey. He is now working on a sequel, an account of a hitchhiking trek through Britain looking for directions. It took him from The Lizard (in the South-West) to Dunnet Head (in the North-East) and his troubles aren't over yet.

You can contact the author by email at:

laurence@thetispublications.co.uk
or www.thetispublications.co.uk

About the Illustrators

HILARY PAYNTER studied sculpture and wood engraving at Portsmouth College of Art. Following careers as a teacher and educational psychologist, she has been a linchpin in the revival of the Society of Wood Engravers, organising exhibitions and latterly as Chairman.

Her prodigious output ranges from dramatic landscapes and pastoral scenes to domestic observations and subtle or savage comment on socio-political matters. Her work is in the collections of the Ashmolean (Oxford), Fitzwilliam (Cambridge) and Victoria & Albert Museums; in city galleries including Birmingham and Portsmouth; in the universities of London and Northumbria.

To commemorate the 250th anniversary of Thomas Bewick, inventor of wood engraving, Hilary was commissioned to produce a suite of wood engravings *From the Rivers to the Sea*. Enlarged and extending over 22 metres, this was installed on the Metro platforms at the Central Station, Newcastle. In 2006, she was elected President of the Royal Society of Painter-Printmakers.

GERRARD LINDLEY has been a freelance graphic illustrator and fine artist since 1977. He has held numerous solo exhibitions since both in Yorkshire and the South West, with work in private collections in America, Denmark, Germany, Spain and Australia.

His subject matter ranges from dance and show business to dreams and the surreal, themes sometimes developed with mixed media constructions incorporating found materials. These are regularly exhibited in the Burton Art Gallery, Bideford.

He lives in Appledore, North Devon, his home serving as an open studio. Having lectured in graphic illustration and run art workshops in the past, he currently supplements his creative career working with people who have learning disabilities.